The Real Winnie

A One-of-a-Kind Bear

Val Shushkewich

NATURAL HERITAGE BOOKS

TORONTO

Published by Natural Heritage / Natural History Inc.
P.O. Box 95, Station O, Toronto, Ontario M4A 2M8

www.naturalheritagebooks.com

National Library of Canada Cataloguing in Publication

Shushkewich, Val, 1950-
      The real Winnie : a one-of-a-kind bear / Val Shushkewich. — 1st ed.

Includes bibliographical references and index.
ISBN 1-896219-89-6

1. Winnipeg (Bear) 2. Colebourn, Harry. 3. Winnie-the-Pooh (Fictitious character) 4. Black bear — Biography. 5. World War, 1914-1918 — Canada. I. Title.

QL737.C27S58 2003   599.78'5'0929   C2003-905074-2

Front cover photo: Captain Harry Colebourn with his cub "Winnie" at the Salisbury Plain. *Courtesy of the Provincial Archives of Manitoba, Colebourn D. Harry 8 Collection, No. N10466.*

Back cover photos: Painting of *Winnie the Pooh and the Honey Pot*, reproduced with permission of Partners in the Park Museum. The Winnie statue in White River, Ontario, courtesy of the Township of White River.

Cover and text design by Sari Naworynski
Edited by Jane Gibson and Melissa Hughes
Printed and bound in Canada by Hignell Book Printing, Winnipeg, Manitoba

THE CANADA COUNCIL | LE CONSEIL DES ARTS
FOR THE ARTS | DU CANADA
SINCE 1957 | DEPUIS 1957

ONTARIO ARTS COUNCIL
CONSEIL DES ARTS DE L'ONTARIO

Natural Heritage / Natural History Inc. acknowledges the financial support of the Canada Council for the Arts and the Ontario Arts Council for our publishing program. We acknowledge the support of the Government of Ontario through the Ontario Media Development Corporation's Ontario Book Initiative. We also acknowledge the financial support of the Government of Canada through the Book Publishing Industry Development Program (BPIDP) and the Association for the Export of Canadian Books.

To my husband Ken

And to the memory of Winnie, who gave so much

Contents

Acknowledgements

We gratefully acknowledge the assistance provided by CWO Gordon Crossley, Museum Director of The Fort Garry Horse Museum and Archives, housed in the McGregor Armoury in Winnipeg. Gordon provided a wealth of background information and education on the life and times of Veterinary Officer Harry Colebourn and on Winnie the Bear.

As well, the assistance of Glenn Wright, historian and archivist at the National Library and Archives of Canada, in verifying Colebourn's military record and detail on the First World War was invaluable. We thank you. Much appreciation goes to Terry Delaney, Curator of the White River Heritage Museum, and to Marilyn Parent Lethbridge, Clerk Administrator for the Corporation of the Township of White River, for their co-operation and support in providing details on the White River portion of this story. We thank Donna Hicks, Executive Director of Partners in the Park in Winnipeg and her colleagues, for providing photographs.

Appreciation also goes to David Friesen of Winnipeg, who was instrumental in furnishing background information on the happenings in his city that relate to Winnie. To Geoff and Lucille Campey of Dinton, near Salisbury, England, go thanks for their supportive research regarding the Salisbury Plain.

The author would also like to thank her parents, Irene and George Cuffe of Winnipeg, for their assistance with the book. Thanks also to Ellen Leroe, an author living in San Francisco, who encouraged this publication. A special thank you goes to Melissa Hughes and Jane Gibson of Natural Heritage Books for their editorial support.

All possible care has been taken to trace the copyright holders of the materials used in this book and to acknowledge same. While many people provided assistance with research, the responsibility for accuracy rests with the author and publisher. Any errors brought to their attention will be rectified in subsequent editions.

Introduction

This is a true account of two lives – one man and one bear – and how their coming together almost a hundred years ago led to a remarkable story, one that is still celebrated today. One of the lives is that of a black bear who became famous in her own lifetime, then immortalized through the writings of A.A. Milne, the creator of the series of children's stories revolving around "Winnie the Pooh." The other life is that of a gentle, caring man named Harry Colebourn, a veterinarian and a military officer without whose love for and kindness to animals, a generation of children may well have been deprived of their lovable, furry, honey-eating friend.

The story begins in 1914. At that time black bears were numerous in Northern Ontario and often were hunted, both for food and for their fur. Sometimes in the spring season, a hunter would shoot a female bear only to discover that she had one or more young cubs. The young animals would not understand what had happened and would be helpless without their mother. Frequently they would not display any fear of the hunter and they would sometimes even follow him around, latching on instinctively to the only large, living mammal in sight. Young cubs, removed from the care of their mother, before she could teach them the necessary skills, were unlikely to survive in the wilds.

In the case of our story, a female black bear had been shot by a hunter in the summer of 1914. Of her two cubs born earlier that year, the surviving one was found by a trapper and brought into White River, a small community in Northern Ontario, Canada. By some quirk of fate, the trapper and the bear cub were at the White River Railway Station when Lieutenant Harry Colebourn's train arrived from Winnipeg. He would not leave the station that day without her.

The story, however, not only involves those lives; it takes place against the backdrop of the First World War, often referred to as The Great War. It is the call to serve in active duty that takes Harry Colebourn to White River and ultimately to the Salisbury Plain in England. Winnie travels in a train carrying soldiers and horses, sails on a troopship and lives in military training camps. Again, it is a call to serve on the battlefields of France that leads to Harry's donating her to the London Zoo. It is there that A.A. Milne and his son Christopher first meet and come under the spell of this Canadian bear.

In the author's telling of the story of Winnie and Harry Colebourn, readers are reminded of some of the key events and individuals who represent Canada's involvement with the Allied forces in this long and tragic conflict of 1914-1918.[1] For those who were fortunate enough to encounter Winnie, the experience would have been one of the few "bright" moments of this difficult time.

1: The Stage Is Set

HARRY COLEBOURN was born in 1887 and raised in Birmingham, Warwickshire, England. That same year, in Canada, the land that was to become his home, the Canadian Pacific Railway was a scant two years old. Its construction had led to the creation of a stopover point in Northern Ontario known as White River. Out in the midwest, Manitoba was a young province, having just been established in July 1870. Winnipeg, its fledgling capital, was welcoming a steady flow of immigrants. Both communities were to become significant in the life of this man - along with a Canadian-born black bear.

During his youth Harry worked as a stable manager for some wealthy landowners, gaining valuable experience for his later career as a veterinarian. He was raised in a family where both love for and kindness to animals were highly valued and these beliefs became very much part of the way he conducted his life. In the words of Fred Colebourn, Harry's son, "My father was such a kind, gentle man. He used to say you could tell a lot about someone by the way they treated animals."[1] By adulthood, Harry had matured into a handsome, fair-complexioned, blue-eyed young man with light brown hair.[2]

From his early years, Harry aspired to become a veterinary surgeon. In 1905, at the age of eighteen, he decided to move to Canada, following his two sisters who had emigrated there some years earlier. Initially he settled in Toronto, Ontario, and,

A formal photograph of D. Harry Colebourn, at the age of twenty-three, demonstrating his affinity for animals, 1910. *Courtesy of the Provincial Archives of Manitoba, Colebourn, D. Harry Collection, N10313.*

determined to follow his dream, he took on a variety of odd jobs, from selling fruit as a street vendor to working as a deckhand on Great Lakes ships,[3] in order to earn enough money for his tuition. It took him three determined years to reach his goal. In the fall of 1908, he was accepted into the Ontario Veterinary College, then part of the University of Toronto and located on Temperance Street in the downtown section of the city.[4] On April 25, 1911, he graduated with the degree of Bachelor of Veterinary Science (BVSc.).

After a brief trip home to England to visit his family, Harry embarked on his chosen career. He accepted a veterinary appointment with the Department of Agriculture and moved to Winnipeg, Manitoba. This city, established at the confluence of the Red and Assiniboine rivers, began life as La Fourche or the Forks, the site of an 18th-century fur trading post that, by 1821 was Fort Garry, part of the Hudson's Bay Company, and later named Winnipeg. The word is taken from the Cree name given to the lake to the north, and means "win" for muddy and "nipee" for water. For thousands of years the land was home to First Nations people.

Located in southern Manitoba, south of Lake Winnipeg and just some ninety-six kilometres (sixty miles) north of the boundary line between Canada and the United States, Winnipeg is almost midway between the Atlantic and Pacific oceans. By the time of Harry's arrival there, the railway had brought in thousands of settlers from around the world. Homesteads grew into extensive farmlands as the vast prairie grasses gave way to the cultivation of wheat. Then, although farm equipment was becoming more mechanized, the horsepower required to work the fields still came in the form of horses — multiple teams of horses. Veterinarians were very much in demand.

A period of unprecedented growth and prosperity that would last for some thirty years was underway. This new rail line, connecting Winnipeg to Toronto and the eastern part of Canada, had opened up new markets, and was introducing a steady stream of travel and trade. An influx of population followed and Winnipeg was rapidly becoming one of Canada's major urban centres. Immigrants from all over Europe and North America continued to flock to the city. When Harry Colebourn took up his new appointment, Winnipeg's population had grown to 136,000.

Once settled in his new home, Harry assumed his veterinary role as part of the Health of Animals section of the Manitoba Department of Agriculture. Like many of the young men of his time, he spent his free time in militia training. On May 15, 1912, he was seconded to the 34th Regiment of Cavalry, later renamed the 34th Fort Garry Horse. By late May of 1913, Harry was recommended for an appointment as a Provisional Lieutenant in the Veterinary Corps. It is interesting to see that this recommendation was signed by the legendary Sir Samuel Steele, the Colonel and Officer Commanding Military District 10. By the outbreak of the First World War in August of 1914, Harry was already a trained officer and ready for service overseas.

Harry Colebourn, age 24, in his graduation photograph. He received his Bachelor of Veterinary Science degree from the Ontario Veterinary College, at that time located in Toronto, Ontario. *Courtesy of Lindsay Mattick, great-grand-daughter of Harry Colebourn.*

Dated May 22, 1913, this document from Harry Colebourn's militia file, pre-dating the outbreak of the First World War, confirms his initial appointment as an officer in the Veterinary Corps. *Courtesy of the National Archives of Canada, Harry Colebourn service record, RG 150, acc. 92-93/166, box 1844.*

Sir Samuel Steele

The legendary Sir Samuel Steele came to personify the Victorian's ideal of the heroic "man of action," first in his role as staff commander with the North West Mounted Police (NWMP), and later as a prominent recruiter and trainer of troops in the First World War. Photos of Steele show a steely-eyed, barrel-chested man; he was known by his contemporaries to be both strong and courageous. Born in Ontario, in Medonte township in Simcoe County, in 1849, Steele's administration was characterized by his systematic attention to detail. Despite romantic notions provoked by the image of the NWMP's "frontiersmen," ready to jump on horseback and ride into unknown territory, Steele was methodical in his approach, almost scientifically surveying a situation before taking action.

The son of a former naval officer, then a member of Parliament, Sam Steele was drawn into the militia by the Fenian uprising of 1866. When he heard in 1873 that the government was planning to form the NWMP, he eagerly signed up for service. He was assigned to the rank of staff constable, taking up his post in October when the first contingent arrived at Lower Fort Garry (now Winnipeg). Steele himself acknowledged that his greatest talent was for training

recruits. He was called upon to exercise this talent many times in his role with the NWMP, and later in the First World War. The outbreak of the Great War found Steele, then 63 years old, with hopes to command the First Canadian Division. However, he was not promoted until December 1914, and then as a major general in charge of training in Western Canada. Thus, his signature is found on the paper recommending Harry Colebourn for promotion in 1914.

Steele did head the Second Canadian Division before it left for France, handling its organization in Canada and training in England, but did not go to the battlefields — he was believed to be too old to command troops in active combat. He was offered a non-combat post as commanding officer of the Southeastern District of England, and later placed in charge of all Canadian troops in England by Sam Hughes, Minister of Defense in Canada. When Hughes fell from power in November 1916, Steele was relieved of his post, after refusing to return to Canada as a recruiter. He was retired on July 15, 1918, and succumbed the following year to the influenza epidemic, just after his 70th birthday. He is buried in Winnipeg in St. John's Cemetery.[5]

On August 23, 1914, Harry Colebourn left Winnipeg, bound for Valcartier, Quebec, the site chosen to be an interim staging area before the Canadian troops were sent overseas to England. While en route, he was detached from the 34th Fort Garry Horse and transferred to the Canadian Army Veterinary Corps (CAVC).

The troop train carrying both Canadian soldiers and the numerous horses destined to haul army wagons and loads of ammunition, as well as provide mounts for the cavalry, was scheduled to stop at White River, Ontario.

2: At the White River Railway Station

THE TOWN OF WHITE RIVER, Ontario, was founded by the Canadian Pacific Railway (CPR) in 1885, part of a rail line construction linking Winnipeg to eastern Canada. Located along the north shore of Lake Superior, roughly midway between Thunder Bay and Sault Ste. Marie, the town is set in the Canadian Shield – a vast rocky boreal forest ecosystem that occupies much of Northern Ontario and Quebec. Here the climate is harsh, especially in the winter. White River was once known as the coldest spot in Canada, a title that put the community on the map.

The extensive rocky terrain of the Shield presented a huge challenge to the railway builders. However, there was no choice. The only route was through Northern Ontario with its huge expanse of rocky outcroppings. Moreover, the distance between Sault Ste. Marie and Thunder Bay was so great that a stopover point was required. William Van Horne, President of the Canadian Pacific Railway, chose the perfect spot for this midway stop, a tiny settlement he referred to as "Snowbank." Here, its low altitude made the natural flow of water to the community relatively simple, ensuring an ample supply of the water that would be required for the trains. Up to this time, the key activities of this tiny community centred around the fur trade, with the exchange of goods that took place between the Hudson's Bay Company, and a few independent companies, and the local Aboriginal people, the Ojibwe.[1]

White River grew out of this CPR divisional point of 1885 into a fully equipped destination for travellers, with a deluxe station house, fine hotels, and an icehouse kept stocked with ice cut from nearby Picnic Lake. A sizeable stockyard was maintained to feed and water all the livestock that were regularly transported on the railway. In 1886, White River supported a population of ten families, but by 1906 there were three churches[2] and the community had grown to forty-two families, becoming a small town servicing the needs of an expanding railway centre.

White River soon emerged as an distinct railway town in the railway era of Canada's history. Positioned as the halfway point stop between Winnipeg and Toronto, all trains stopped there to take on coal and water. During the First World War, most troop trains also carried horses for cavalry troops and for the transport of guns and munitions at the front. At the White River stop, the animals were taken off the train to be fed, watered and exercised. Troop trains stopped here for four to six hours, allowing both animals and soldiers an extended break in their journey.

On August 24, 1914, a troop train from Winnipeg bound for Quebec stopped at White River. Lieutenant Harry Colebourn was the veterinarian officer in charge of the horses being transported on board. One of the first things to catch his eye when

In the book *White River – 100 Years, Pictorial History*, this photograph is identified as a "Circus Day," and credited to G. Carlson.[3] It is believed to have been a July 1st celebration, c. 1911. *Courtesy of the Township of White River.*

An early photograph of the community of White River, taken from across the river, looking towards the town, not dated. *Courtesy of the Township of White River.*

he disembarked at the station, was a solitary trapper sitting on a bench. A little black bear cub was tethered to the armrest. Perhaps it was Harry's love of animals that caused him to stop. But for whatever reason he took an immediate interest and sat down on the bench with the odd pair. The trapper told him that the cub was the surviving one of twins, and that he had shot the mother. It seems that Harry intuitively discovered something so charming and loveable about the little cub that he decided he would adopt her right away. Fortunately, Colebourn was meticulous in keeping a journal. His daily entry documenting the occasion reads, "August 24, 1914. Left Port Arthur 7A. In train all day. Bought bear. $20."[4] A later journal notation identifies the town as White River. Some years afterwards, Harry's son, Fred, would comment on this fortuitous meeting: "He (my father) knew it was a one-of-a-kind bear. Special. But I don't think he knew what would happen in the end."[5]

When Harry suggested the hefty sum of $20 for the cub (worth about $360 today), the offer was gladly accepted. This time when Colebourn re-boarded the train, he was accompanied by the little black bear. He called her "Winnipeg Bear," after Winnipeg in Manitoba, Canada, the city where he had settled as a veterinarian. Later he shortened the name to simply "Winnie."

A photograph of the Canadian Pacific Railway station at White River taken July 22, 1911, by civil engineer J.W. Heckman. Note the extensive umbrella-type platform roof. *The photo, originally from the Canadian Pacific Railway Corporate Archives, is courtesy of the White River Heritage Museum.*

Winnie was an *Ursus americanus* or American black bear, the most common of the species of bears in North America. Found in wooded areas in many parts of Canada, the United States and Mexico, black bears can survive in varied habitats and climates. When compared to other species of bears, a full-grown black bear is only medium-sized and most adults are five to six feet tall when standing and weigh between 300 and 500 pounds. Black bears roamed the forests of North America long before the Native Americans. And, unlike many animal species that were common at that time, black bear populations remain strong today with estimates of about 400,000 to 750,000 of the bears living in the wild.[6]

Folklore of Bears

Bears have figured heavily in the mythology of many cultures, and rightly so: studies have revealed that these mammals, particularly American black bears, may be among the world's most intelligent. Their reputation for cunning and trickery — hunters tell of bears muffling their trails by walking in streambeds, or even in their own tracks — may have led to the sense of mystery that has historically surrounded these powerful animals. Even today, the bear is central to the spirituality of Native Peoples; many believe them to have healing properties, and to possess powers over life and death.

One legend, which has many variations amongst tribes, tells of a child who is abandoned in the wilderness by a wayward caregiver only to be rescued from certain starvation by a family of bears and reared among them. Traditionally, the bear has also been a symbol of rebirth, due to its hibernation through the winter months and its reappearance in the spring, which must have seemed a miracle to early peoples. In fact, shamans, who were thought to be able to channel the spirit world, often chose to adorn themselves in bear skins, claws and teeth, believing them to have healing properties. To cure the sick, a shaman would invoke the spirit of a bear, or touch the afflicted person with the claw of the animal.[7]

The black bear, native to North America, is believed to be among the world's most intelligent mammals. *Photo by R.D. Lawrence.*

Humans have always been a major predator of the black bear and during the settlement of North America, bears were frequently hunted. Bear fat was commonly used as cooking oil, bearskins provided warmth and even bear meat was considered a delicacy. By 1914, it was not uncommon for black bears to be sought for their pelts, many of which were used to make bearskin hats for the Grenadier Guards.

In Winnie's case, the little black bear cub was only about seven months old when she first encountered Harry Colebourn. Fortunately, the individual who had shot her mother, had not abandoned her in the woods. She would not have lived left on her own. It was sheer serendipity that this man, whose name is not recorded, had the bear cub at the White River Station at precisely the time that Harry Colebourn's train pulled in to the station. It was this military officer, a veterinarian with a special love for animals, who was to adopt and care for her at a time in her life when she was in desperate need.

3: En Route to England

THE CARING RELATIONSHIP between the Canadian officer and his newly acquired bear cub began to develop over the next two days as they travelled together on a troop train bound for Quebec. The train arrived at Valcartier at seven o'clock on the morning of August 26, 1914. Immediately both officers and those of other ranks proceeded to pitch their tents and establish sick lines to tend to the horses in their care. An outbreak of influenza among the thousands of horses acquired for overseas duty created an immediate need for veterinary services.[1]

Harry Colebourn was part of Canada's huge early mobilization of the first contingent of fighting forces to serve in The Great War. As a member of the British Commonwealth, Canada had automatically become a party to the conflict when Britain declared war on Germany, on August 4, 1914. Citizens from across the land responded quickly. Within forty-eight hours of the declaration of war, formal authority was given for the calling up of the Canadian Expeditionary Force. Twenty thousand volunteers were needed. Within two weeks, more than thirty thousand volunteer recruits had enlisted. Engineers were immediately deployed to build a camp for the mobilization and training of soldiers at Valcartier, twenty-seven kilometres (sixteen miles) to the west of Quebec City. In less than three weeks, a rudimentary military encampment was in full operation. A waterworks system, a telephone system and an electric

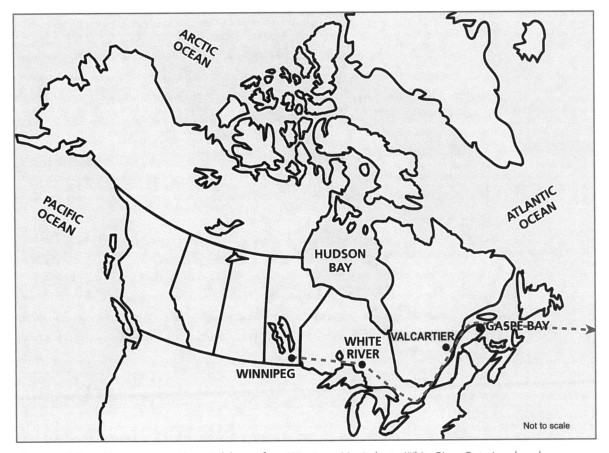

The route followed by Lieutenant Harry Colebourn from Winnipeg, Manitoba, to White River, Ontario, where he acquired Winnie in August 1914. From White River, the Canadian troops travelled by rail to Valcartier and, in late September, sailed from Quebec City en route to England as part of the Canadian Expeditionary Force. *Courtesy of Val Shushkewich.*

light system were all installed. Troughs of drinking water for horses filled automatically, so that there was neither shortage nor waste. A line of rifle targets three-and-a-half-miles long, the largest rifle range in the world, was constructed.[2] Altogether, the Canadian Expeditionary Force was mobilized in less than two months. It was an incredible effort to plan and execute this large-scale troop movement and to organize a training site in such a short time.

Declaration of War – First World War

The assassination of Archduke Franz Ferdinand (heir to the Austrian throne) was the spark igniting a series of events in Europe that eventually caused Britain to declare war on Germany on August 4th, 1914. As a member of the British Commonwealth, Canada was automatically at war. Canadians rushed to pledge their support for the Mother Country, lining up to enlist at recruiting offices in astounding numbers. Indeed, only weeks after Prime Minister Robert Borden offered his country's assistance to the Commonwealth, an expeditionary force of 32,000 men (which included Harry Colebourn of Winnipeg and Winnie the Bear) of the Canadian Army Veterinary Corps had been assembled at Valcartier Camp near Quebec City. Two months later, they set sail for England and a winter of hard training.

In December 1914, the first Canadian troops, Princess Patricia's Canadian Light Infantry, arrived in France. The 1st Canadian Division followed in February 1915. What had begun as the colony's regular peacetime army of only 3,110, would swell by war's end to a massive force of more than 600,000 Canadians in uniform. Sir Wilfrid Laurier captured the mood of the majority of Canadians when he proclaimed: "It is our duty to let Great Britain know and to let the friends and foes of Great Britain know that there is in Canada but one mind and one heart and that all Canadians are behind the Mother County."[3] Four years later, Canada would emerge from The Great War mortally wounded – having suffered nearly a quarter of a million casualties – but with a newfound national identity and pride in the participation of its citizens.

With over 9,000 horses in the Valcartier Camp, a field veterinary hospital was established. Staffed by the Winnipeg Section of the CAVC, Harry Colebourn, as one of the five officers, played a key role. Hundreds of serious cases of disease and injury were treated successfully, and the horses returned to their respective units. The necessary veterinary equipment and supplies were purchased at Ottawa and Quebec and each veterinary officer was issued quantities deemed sufficient for overseas duty.[4]

On September 12, 1914, Harry became part of the Second Canadian Infantry Brigade Headquarters under the command of Lieutenant Colonel Arthur W. Currie, the man who ultimately became the commander of the Canadian Expeditionary Force in the First World War.

Sir Arthur W. Currie

An important, although controversial, character in Canadian military history, Arthur Currie headed up Canadian forces in France during the First World War, becoming the first Canadian to hold the rank of General. Currie has been lauded by historians for his efforts to visit Canadian troops on the front and to keep them united in a single Canadian division, as well as for his planning and execution of the Battle of Vimy Ridge in 1917 – the battle that many feel gave recognition to Canada as a nation. He was knighted by King George V in 1917.

There has, however, been criticism of Currie's leadership, specifically for ordering troops to action at Mons – in which several men died – just hours before the 1918 Armistice. It has also been suggested that, in order to pay off his own debts, he diverted money from the regiment's funds.[5]

Born on his family's farm at Napperton, near Strathroy, Ontario, in 1875, Currie later became Principal and Vice-Chancellor of McGill University and held the position until his death in 1933. Despite the controversy surrounding his military career, Currie remains a pivotal figure in our war history, and a man of great interest to scholars.

Arthur W. Currie (1875-1933), from southwestern Ontario, became the first Canadian in The Great War to achieve the rank of General. *Courtesy of the National Archives of Canada / PA-001370.*

At Valcartier, Winnie the Bear soon became a great favourite of Currie and indeed of all the men of the Infantry Brigade. Already she was considered the official mascot of the veterinary corps.[6] The soldiers grew to love Winnie's playful antics and gentle nature during the time they spent with her, both in training at the Valcartier Camp and later at the training site for Canadian soldiers on the Salisbury Plain in England. By now, Winnie had adapted to her human surroundings under the kind and gentle care of Harry Colebourn, and was developing into an outgoing, friendly creature. The men took delight in her presence and included her in both their group and individual photographs.

Harry and Winnie stayed at Valcartier for only a very short time. On September 24, 1914, he wrote in his diary that he was "making preparations to leave Canada."[7] Interestingly, Harry's promotion to the rank of Captain is shown in his war record as dating from September 25, 1914.[8] By then a huge force was assembled at Quebec.

EN ROUTE TO ENGLAND

15

A group photograph of Section 10, Canadian Army Veterinary Corps, Winnipeg, at Valcartier. Note the bell tents behind. "Identifiable are Lieut. C.E. Edgett, middle row, second from right, and Lieut. Harry Colebourn, middle row, second from left. Officer seated middle row with Stetson hat is probably [Capt.] H.J. Elliot. On the ground front fourth from the left is Cpl. G.I. Brodie. Bear cub 'Winnie' is in the lap of the man to the right of Brodie. This group illustrates pre-W.W.I khaki Service Dress, with three types of hat, the Navy still forage cap, the Stetson, ... and the cork helmet covered with khaki cloth."[9] *Courtesy of the Provincial Archives of Manitoba, Colebourn, D. Harry 19 Collection, No. N10477.*

The embarkation, begun on September 23, continued for eight days with the incomplete state of the stalls for the horses hindering the work of loading the animals. However, all were embarked without casualty.[10] Thirty merchant ships had hurriedly been prepared for their troop transport roles and organized to carry 1,547 officers, 29,070 men, 7,657 horses, 70 guns, 110 motor vehicles, 705 horsed vehicles and 82 bicycles across the Atlantic.[11]

Captain Harry Colebourn, along with Winnie, embarked on the *S.S. Manitou* on the afternoon of September 28, 1914, and sailed from Quebec City. The plan was for the convoy of ships to move down the St. Lawrence and assemble at Gaspé Bay, on the easternmost end of the Gaspé Peninsula. There, the warships that were to escort them across the Atlantic awaited their arrival. The troopships arrived in discreet batches – three on September 29, thirteen on October 1, twelve during the day of October 2, and two during the night. Upon arrival at the appointed destination, they anchored in the positions they would hold in the convoy while sailing across the ocean. Information on the rendezvous at Gaspé Bay and on the time of departure for Europe was carefully guarded – disclosed only shortly before leaving and then only to those who needed to know. The inhabitants of the nearby area were also asked not to disclose any information on the ships' movements. By maintaining a shroud of secrecy around the plans, the commanders hoped to keep the troopships safe from German attack.

On October 3, 1914, the entire naval fleet, containing the largest military force that had ever crossed the Atlantic at one time, set sail for England. It was a fine fall day, perfect for their departure. The sight of three parallel rows of about a dozen ships each, with flags flying and signals twinkling, must have been both an impressive and chilling sight for the handful of people who saw them off. The *S.S. Manitou*, with Harry and Winnie on board, was in the middle of this convoy. Winnie, however, was never to return to Canada.

Four cruisers and a battleship, with a second one joining during the passage across the Atlantic, provided the escort. Originally, the troops were to disembark at Southampton, but after two German submarines were spotted dangerously close to the vicinity, the ships were diverted to Plymouth, a major port city more westerly on the southern coast of England. Fears for the convoy's safety were justified: two enemy submarines sighted on October 12 and 13 in the approach to Southampton had been dispatched from Germany specifically to attack this fleet. It appears that spies in New York had informed the German Admiralty on October 8 as to the movements of the Canadian fleet, and their military authorities issued orders to attack.[12] Interestingly, intelligence had reported that twenty-four transports, escorted by eight warships, had left Quebec on October 2, which was almost exactly accurate! However, as the Germans had believed that the Canadian troops were sufficiently trained to be taken directly to the battlefield, Boulogne, France, was assumed to be their destination;

they were expected to arrive between October 10th and 12th. Luckily for the convoy, neither of the two German submarines dispatched off Boulogne came as far west as the port at Plymouth, and the ships escaped attack. The military intelligence for the Allies[13] was wise to have taken the threat of a German submarine attack seriously.

By 1912, the German military had seriously begun to build their submarine fleet as instruments of war. On the eve of the First World War, the art of submarine warfare was barely a dozen years old. No nation had developed any method to detect and

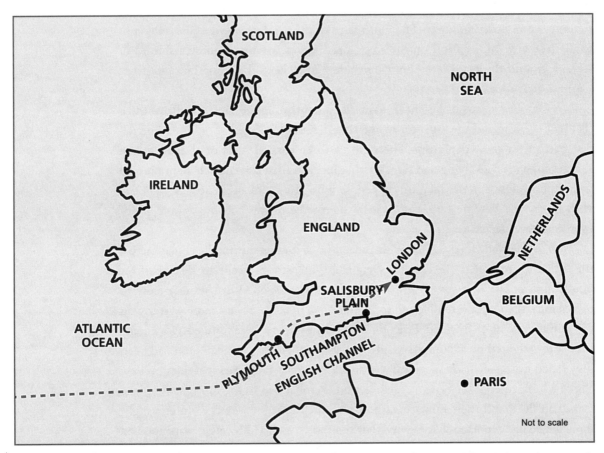

A map showing the destination of the Canadian convoy at Plymouth, England; the location of the Salisbury Plain, site of the military training camps, and the ultimate route taken by Harry Colebourn and Winnie on their way to the London Zoo. *Courtesy of Val Shushkewich.*

destroy enemy submarines. As the world's greatest naval power at the outset of the war, Great Britain had the largest submarine fleet of any nation, but Germany, even with its late start in establishing its fleet, was considered to have the most capable.

As soon as war broke out in August 1914, both the British and the Germans sent submarines to observe enemy movements. The fear that troop ships could be torpedoed by German subs proved to be well-founded. In May 1915, the British passenger liner *Lusitania* was sunk by a German U-boat. The German commander is believed to have mistaken the liner for a troopship.[14]

As it turned out, the transatlantic voyage of the First Canadian Expeditionary Force was long, but uneventful. Harry Colebourn was sick for much of the journey and remained in the ship's hospital from the 6th of October to the 13th.[15] No doubt Harry would have entrusted the care of Winnie to a colleague. How the bear cub adapted to her time at sea is not recorded, but she obviously survived the journey, and it is likely that her presence contributed to the entertainment on board the *Manitou*.

So strict had been the censorship on the convoy's movements that the arrival of the Canadian fleet in Plymouth Sound was quite unexpected by the residents of the area. However, no sooner had the word gone out that the Canadian transports had docked that the townsfolk flocked to the waterside to cheer the newcomers. No one was allowed on board, but on succeeding days when the troops landed and marched through the streets, they received a warm welcome.

Harry and Winnie departed the *S.S. Manitou* on October 17, leaving Devonport at seven o'clock that evening, bound for further training on British soil – their destination, the Salisbury Plain.

4: On the Salisbury Plain

THE SALISBURY PLAIN, in the southwest of England, is a rolling chalk plateau dominated by large arable fields. It is home to the ancient monument of Stonehenge. The extent of the plain itself is an outstanding prehistoric ritual landscape, containing many conspicuous and widespread earthworks and monuments that are prominent in the open landscape.

In 1914, Salisbury Plain was the main training ground of the British army and troops from the Commonwealth, including soldiers from Australia, New Zealand and South Africa, as well as those from Canada. Much of its territory became clusters of tents – a veritable tented city. The Canadian forces occupied camps at West Down South, West Down North, Pond Farm, Lark Hill and Sling Plantation. This grouping of camps offered an almost perfect training area in the summer months. However, shortly after the First Canadian Expeditionary Force arrived, the weather changed dramatically and a continual downpour of rain began. In what was to prove to be a grim foreshadowing of the conditions the men would endure in France, there followed one of the worst winters on record in England. The rain poured down day after day, making the roads virtually impassable. The low plateau became a morass of mud. Everything from tents to clothes, including tobacco and matches, became saturated with water. Even rudimentary training was nearly impossible in the unrelenting weather. At night the men were forced to sleep in soggy, chilling blankets. It is little wonder that morale was at an all-time low. The one spot of joy throughout during these dismal days was Winnie. Seemingly impervious to the rain, she was a welcome sight, bringing some fun to otherwise dismal days.

During the two months that Captain Colebourn and Winnie spent on the Salisbury Plain, he nurtured the bear's playful, gentle nature. As Harry took personal responsibility for her feeding and general care, Winnie stayed in his tent. At night, she slept under his cot. The black bear cub was taught numerous tricks, and is reported to have played many games with the men. She liked to shimmy up the centre pole in Harry's tent and give it a shake. However, as she matured, taking on both weight and girth during the weeks of training on the Salisbury Plain, it became a concern that her antics might accidentally collapse the temporary shelter. Consequently, the men erected a special pole outside Harry's tent for her to climb.

In addition to fulfilling her role as mascot, Winnie quickly became a "pet" to many of the soldiers. Like a puppy, she would follow them around in their off-duty hours, participating in their hijinks. It seems that her playful, accepting nature and willingness to please were apparent to the men, and her constantly gentle nature was especially endearing. Her presence helped take their minds off their ongoing soggy circumstances and off the

A serious-looking Captain Harry Colebourn, with his bear cub Winnie, 1914. *Courtesy of the Provincial Archives of Manitoba, Colebourn, D. Harry 10 Collection, No. N10468.*

prospect of the conflict to come. Group photographs frequently included Winnie, front and centre, a position of honour.

As for Winnie, she seemed to consider herself as being no different from all the human animals in whose company she found herself. No doubt, this love of human company was the result of the young Winnie having imprinted on Colebourn.[1]

It is often observed that the "master" is a mirror for his "animal" and it seems apparent that Harry's warm, playful nature was passed on to Winnie, and reflected in her legendary nose for games and fun. In merriment, Harry Colebourn was most certainly no slouch. He was known around camp to have quite an engaging sense of humour, as can be seen in "The Soldier's Ten Commandments." It is believed that he may have penned these lines while at Salisbury:

"The Pet" Winnie on the Salisbury Plain, 1914. Photo by A.F. Marett, Shrewton. *Courtesy of the Provincial Archives of Manitoba, Colebourn, D. Harry 11 Collection, No. N10469.*

(1) When on guard thou shalt challenge all parties approaching thee.
(2) Thou shalt not send any engraving nor any likeness of any airship in heaven above, nor any postcard of the earth beneath, nor of any submarine in the sea, for I, the Censor am a jealous Censor, visiting iniquities of the offenders with three months C.B. but showing mercy unto thousands by letters, the letters go first of those who obey my commandments.
(3) Thou shalt not use profuse language unless, under extraordinary circumstances, such as seeing thy mate snore, or getting petrol in thy tea.
(4) Remember the soldier's week consists of seven days, six days shalt thou labour and on the seventh day thou shalt do all odd jobs.
(5) Honour thy King and country, keep thy rifle clean, and shoot straight that thy days may be long in the land the army giveth thee.

(6) Thou shalt not steal thy comrade's kit.

(7) Thou shalt not kill time.

(8) Thou shalt not adulterate thy mess tin by using it as a shaving mug.

(9) Thou shalt not hear false witness against thy comrade, but reserve silence on his out-goings and in-comings.

(10) Thou shalt not covet thy Corporal's post neither Sergeant Major's, but by thy duty and perseverance thou shalt rise to the position of Field Marshall."[2]

Winnie, front centre, with officers of the Second Canadian Infantry Brigade in front of a cluster of tents at a training camp on the Salisbury Plain, 1914. *Courtesy of the Provincial Archives of Manitoba, Colebourn, D. Harry 20 Collection, No. N10478.*

Winnie with an unidentified veterinary officer and his horse pose for a photographer on the Salisbury Plain, 1914. Note the caked mud on the man's boots and on the horse's hooves. *Courtesy of the Provincial Archives of Manitoba, Colebourn, D. Harry 13 Collection, No. N10471.*

Winnie's days as mascot to the Second Canadian Infantry Brigade on the Salisbury Plain were coming to a close. A dispatch was soon to arrive that would alter the relationship between Harry and Winnie forever.

With the encampment at Salisbury Plain in the background, Winnie and Captain Harry Colebourn appear to be enjoying some time together, 1914. *Courtesy of the Provincial Archives of Manitoba, Colebourn, D. Harry Collection, No. N10467.*

5 : First Days at the London Zoo

WINNIE'S LIFE WITH Captain Colebourn and the Second Canadian Infantry Brigade was to be short-lived. In early December, Harry was given orders to remove Winnie from the Brigade Headquarters, in anticipation of their imminent departure for France. It was clear that Winnie could not accompany him to the battlefields. On December 9, 1914, Harry somehow acquired a motorcar, loaded Winnie as his passenger, and drove off, headed for the City of London.

Winnie was less than a year old, a perfectly tame and very friendly black bear, but also mischievous; it is said that Winnie tried to escape from the car on the way to the Zoo. The handsome young soldier and his furry companion must have been an interesting pair, as they made their way across the countryside and into the heart of the city.

The London Zoo is the best-known zoo in Britain, with one of the most famous and prestigious collections of animals in the world. Spread over thirty-six acres on the north side of Regent Park, less than two miles from the centre of the city, it is the primary home of the Royal Zoological Society of London. This society was founded in 1826 at the instigation of its first president, Sir Stamford Raffles. The Royal Zoological Society's Gardens opened in 1828 to members of the Society only, and was billed as the world's first scientific centre for animals. Originally, the gardens housed a collection of exotic animals that were studied by eminent scientists of the day. Some animals came from the Royal Menagerie, which had been based for centuries at the Tower of London, while others had been donated by Raffles and by other collectors and scientists. Among the regular visitors at the time was Charles Darwin, who was one of the Members (or Fellows) of the Zoological Society from 1831. His particular fascination was with the orangutan, the first ever seen in Europe.

Sir Stamford Raffles

Sir Thomas Stamford Raffles, British colonial administrator, was born on board a ship at sea off the Island of Jamaica, on July 6, 1781. The vessel was commanded by his father, Benjamin Raffles, a captain in the East Indies trade. Raffles, mostly self-educated, was stationed in Penang (now part of Malaysia) in 1805 as assistant secretary to the governor of the island. He had entered the service of the East India Company at age 14. During the war between Great Britain and France, Raffles paved the way for the British invasion of the Island of Java (now part of Indonesia), which was then ruled by the Dutch.

After a successful campaign, Raffles remained in Java as Lieutenant Governor. When the island was returned to the Dutch in 1816, Raffles returned to England where he published a book based on his knowledge of Java's past. In 1817, he was knighted and appointed Lieutenant Governor of Bencoolen, Sumatra (now Bengkulu, Indonesia). With the purpose of extending British influence into Southeast Asia, he established a settlement on the Island of Singapore.

He died in Barvet, England, on July 5, 1826, and never did see the gardens of the Zoological Society of London.[1]

Initially, there was no intention to admit the general public to the gardens. From its inception, the gates of the gardens were only open to Fellows of the Society and their friends. But within twenty years of its establishment, financial disaster was looming. And so it was, in 1847, that the general public was admitted for the first time on payment of one shilling on weekdays. The exclusive access of Fellows was reduced to Sundays only. This fee would remain unchanged for nearly one hundred years.

The Mappin Terraces enclosure at the London Zoo[2] was the design inspiration of Sir Peter Chalmers Mitchell, the Secretary of the Zoological Society of London from 1903 to 1935. An imitation of a mountain landscape, it was designed to provide a naturalistic habitat for bears and other animals. The primary construction material

A more informal photograph of an unidentified officer and Winnie. As is evident, Winnie was very popular with the men, and they loved to pose with her. Winnie was still a cub, less than a year old, when she left the Canadian training camp for her move to the London Zoo. *Courtesy of the Provincial Archives of Manitoba, Colebourn, D. Harry 13 Collection, No. N10470.*

was reinforced concrete, a comparatively new material at that time.[3] The Mappin Terraces was built in 1913-1914, made possible by a donation from the cutlery and jewellery firm of Mappin & Webb. Jonathan Mappin had opened his first small silversmith workshop in 1774. His business grew steadily and soon the next generation of Mappins was expanding the business even further. In 1897, Mappin & Webb was granted the Royal Warrants for silversmiths to Her Majesty Queen Elizabeth II.

The Mappin Terraces was still considered new when Harry and Winnie first arrived there. Someone may have drawn the veterinarian's attention to an article in *The Guardian Unlimited* of May 26, 1914, describing the movement of zoo animals into the newly finished enclosures as follows:

> This afternoon at the Zoo the keepers were persuading the haughty flamingoes to take up residence in their pond at the foot of the new Mappin terraces. All this week the animals will be walking two by two from their cages to the semi-liberty of the terraces.
>
> About a dozen bears are already there, sniffing about the concrete hillocks, but the bears in the rather dark and confined cages under the old terrace walk have yet to be shifted. Their removal will be the toughest job, for the keepers tell you that you never know when you have a bear. The removal of the goats and other rock-climbing creatures that will inhabit the three mountains at the back will be easy.
>
> Sam and Barbara, the two Polar bears, have been in their compartment since Christmas, and are as happy in it as if they had never lived anywhere else. They have never done anything so foolish as to try and cross the twelve-foot ditch that divides them from the gazers on the terrace. They have a good deep pond at the back, and behind the terraces there is a little window through which you can watch them actually swimming under water.
>
> One imagines that the concrete floor and walls must get unpleasantly hot in summer weather, but the keepers say this is not so. During the recent spell of heat the bears spent most of their time in the water, and rarely visited the cool caves constructed in the concrete

at the back. The black Malaysian bears and the sloths were turned in
a few days ago and are settling down happily.[4]

One can only imagine Harry's thoughts as he handed Winnie to her new care-
givers. Under the circumstances, he had few choices. After all, it was only to be temporary, and Harry would visit his Winnie whenever possible.

It seems that when Winnie was first introduced at the Mappin Terraces, a
Himalayan bear already in the same enclosure at first resented the intrusion of this
strange, Canadian-born bear. However, the two became reconciled in a few days,[5]
when the Himalayan realized that the newcomer would not fight back. The playful
gambols of the new addition to the London Zoo made the Mappin Terraces a more
attractive place for both residents and visitors alike.

Harry had made special arrangements with the London Zoo, placing Winnie on
loan for safekeeping. He planned to return for her once his war duty was over, and
take her back to Canada with him. Actually, Winnie was the first of six black bear
cubs presented to the London Zoo by various contingents of the Canadian Forces

during the beginning of the First World War. However, only Harry Colebourn's Winnie seems to stand out. Her exceptionally good disposition set her apart, casting her as the loveable bear who would captivate not only the hearts of those who saw her, but eventually the imaginations of generations to come.

6: To the Battlefields

AFTER MAKING CERTAIN that Winnie was settled in the London Zoo, Harry Colebourn left the Salisbury Plain with the Second Canadian Infantry Brigade. In early February of 1915 they boarded the train for Avonmouth, their port of embarkation, bound for St. Nazaire, located on the French coast of the Bay of Biscay. Arthur Currie, now a Major General, was in command of this Canadian fighting unit. As was his custom, Harry recorded the events of February 10, 1915, in his diary:

> Left Amesbury 7 a.m. for Avonmouth. Arrived 4 p.m.
> Embarked S.S. Dunkirk (City of Dunkirk).
> Detrained our horses on boat – overnight.
> All horses embarked without mishap.
> Deck hand fell into the water between ship and dock, was rescued.[1]

The last transport reached its destination in the second week of February and Captain Colebourn was assigned as a Veterinary Officer to continue his service with the Canadian Infantry. During the course of the war he undertook duty at the veterinary hospital for sick and wounded animals established at Le Havre on the French side of the English Channel, in addition to the general and medical care of the horses of his

Harry Colebourn
in military
uniform,
circa 1915.
*Courtesy of the
Provincial Archives of
Manitoba, Colebourn,
D. Harry 6 Collection,
No. N10317.*

regiment.[2] Under his command were a number of enlisted and non-commissioned personnel assigned to assist him in carrying out his responsibilities.

During the First World War, horses and mules were essential to military operations as they were needed to transport guns, munitions, and general supplies, and to move the wounded and the dead. When the wagon carts had been pulled as close as possible to the front line trenches, the horses were unhooked, driven back, and the guns hauled by hand to their required positions. From our perspective of the technology of warfare today, it is amazing to look back at the wartime roles of horses and veterinarians. Then, horses were so critical to the military that 75% of the space for supplies sent to France in The Great War was given to hay and other animal necessities.[3]

Veterinary Services during the First World War

The Veterinary Services that were part of the British Imperial Armies were organized in a particular fashion under the control of the Director of Veterinary Services. The Veterinary Service represented to the animals of the army, what the Medical Service was to the troops. Their primary aim was "the reduction to the lowest possible degree of preventable animal wastage."[4] The first duty of the Veterinary Service was to keep the animals fit, which was accomplished by attempting to prevent the introduction of contagious or infectious diseases, and by the prompt treatment of minor ailments, as well as giving advice on the care of the horses in the field. The second duty of the Veterinary Service was to evacuate the horses from the field forces as quickly as possible once they were no longer fit. Veterinary Officers like Harry Colebourn with field units and formations were allotted to the Cavalry regiments, Artillery and Infantry brigades, the Divisional Ammunition column and Divisional Trains. Their duties called for "sound judgment and quick decisions"[5] in rendering first aid in all cases of sickness and injury, and to supervise the care of animals. There were also mobile veterinary sections that were allotted to each Cavalry and Infantry division with the duty of collecting all sick or wounded animals within the formation, and clearing them from the fighting zone as quickly as possible. If the force was stationary, they established hospitals for the care of horses that were likely to recover soon. Severe cases were evacuated from the field for treatment. The Veterinary Hospitals established on the lines of communication for the care of sick and wounded animals were capable of accommodating 1,000 animals.

All army officers were required to be aware of the principles of general veterinary care of their horses and the manual *Veterinary Service, including simple advice and treatment in the field* listed "veterinary hints for common ailments and injuries when veterinary advice is not available,"[6] for such diseases and injuries as ringworm, mange, ticks, tendon sprains, cracked heels and mud fever, bullet wounds, broken knees, cuts and tears, coughs and colds, fever, diarrhea and exhaustion after hard work. It also gave instructions on how to prepare the animals' food – bran mash and steamed oats – and sadly, but necessarily, instructed soldiers in the most humane way to shoot a horse that had to be destroyed.

The Role of the Cavalry in the First World War

Horses have been used in warfare for centuries; World War I marked the end of an era for the animal's role in successful military strategy. The Canadian Cavalry Brigade was formed in December 1914 as part of the First Canadian Contingent. It was originally comprised of the Royal Canadian Horse Artillery, Royal Canadian Dragoons, Lord Strathcona's Horse, and the King Edward's Horse. In February 1916, the latter was replaced by The Fort Garry Horse, to which Harry Colebourn had originally belonged, before his transfer to the Veterinary Corps.

The war presented few opportunities for combat on horseback. By this time, the use of horses and riders had been largely outmoded, although the animals were still needed to haul artillery and heavy machinery. When the Brigade left for France at the latter end of April 1915, it was as a Dismounted Force, playing an important role on foot and in the trenches as infantry.

When the Brigade was returned to a Cavalry Force in 1916, it was pivotal in several military operations; first on the Somme,[7] and later in the fighting at Saulcourt-Guyancourt, where Lieutenant F.M.W. Harvey of Lord Strathcona's Horse received the Victoria Cross after he rushed a machine gun post, capturing it and saving the lives of many under his command. Major H. Strachan of The Fort Garry Horse also received the Cross for his gallant aid of the infantry at Cambrai.

During the Great War, the cavalry still possessed the advantage of increased mobility, and could perform long-range reconnaissance and security for commanders. However, mass charges of horses and riders against infantrymen often ended in horrendous loss of life. As battlefields became increasingly mechanized, tanks and airplanes simply outperformed – and therefore outmoded – mounted troops.

Although mounted cavalry no longer serve an active role in Canada's military, some regiments still serve in dismounted operations. If Harry Colebourn could return to The Fort Garry Horse today, he would find an Armoured Reconnaissance unit in the Canadian Army Reserve, based at McGregor Armoury in Winnipeg, Manitoba.

As part of the Canadian Corps during the First World War, Harry was stationed on the Western Front, a jagged line of trenches dug into the mud and clay of France, stretching approximately 960 kilometres (576 miles) from the Belgian coast to the border of Switzerland. Here armed soldiers faced one another over the shell-torn, muddy and decaying landscape of "No Man's Land."[8] Harry Colebourn and his comrades were confronted daily with the cruel realities of disease and death.[9]

When the First Canadian Expeditionary Force, including Harry, arrived in France, the system of trenches had already been established. To reach the trenches, the soldiers had to come within rifle shot of the enemy. In most places, the German and Allied trenches were not more than 228 metres (250 yards) from each other, and sometimes they were only 36 to 45 metres (40 to 50 yards) apart. To reach the front line trenches, the soldiers had to creep and crawl at dusk, along paths that months of experience had taught them were the best means of approach. These paths led into a communication trench, which, in a number of zigzags, led to the firing trench, where the men were waiting, rifles in hand, in case of attack. This was the Front Line. From 1914 to 1918, the Front Line scarcely moved, crawling forward a few metres at a time, and then only at a tremendous cost in lives and, for many, excruciating wounds. For the veterinarians, it was a very difficult job trying to maintain the horses' health in the appalling conditions behind the Front. The attrition in horses was as bad as, if not worse than, it was for the men. There were terrible outbreaks of equine flu as horses were pushed to the limit all day hauling guns and supplies to the front lines, and pulling wagons containing the dead and injured away from the front lines. At night, the horses often had to be left outside in the cold and wet, with minimal, if any, shelter. The human conditions that surrounded Harry were even more horrifying.

Harry was attached to the Second Canadian Infantry during the famous Second

Horses hauling ammunition wagons during the First World War, 1918.[10]

Battle of Ypres,[11] the outcome of which was bittersweet – more than 6,000 Canadians lost their lives, holding the Allied position on the Western Front that April of 1915. In an effort to create a break in the Allied front, the German forces had launched an asphyxiating chlorine gas attack against a French division, made up of Algerian colonists positioned immediately to the left of the Canadian line. The yellow cloud of fumes, aided by a favourable wind, floated backwards, poisoning and severely disabling all those who fell under its effect, across an extended area along the Front. As a result, the tortured Algerians were compelled to give ground for a considerable distance, thereby opening a gaping hole in the Allied line of defense. The Canadian troops hastily filled the opening to prevent the expected German breakthrough, and held the Allied position against an onslaught of heightened enemy attacks. On April 22 and 23, the Canadians fought all day and all night despite the terrible slaughter in their midst of many of their comrades and commanding officers. Displaying enormous courage, those remaining continued to resist even though the enemy assaults pushed forward with increasing strength.

Although methods for resisting gas attacks were quickly developed, the Canadians at the time were not provided with the proper means for withstanding the fumes. However, it was quickly discovered that a handkerchief drenched with wet mud or urine and stuffed in the mouth protected their lungs, but not their eyes. It would not be until later in the war that gas masks became standard issue for both soldiers and horses. Reinforcements of British troops began to appear in the early morning of April 24, but the fighting continued until the following evening, when all that remained of the decimated but victorious Canadian battalions finally received some relief with the arrival of fresh troops.

The horrors of this battle near Ypres left a lasting impression on the survivors. It is believed to have inspired the famous wartime poem, "In Flanders Fields," written in May of 1915 by Major John McCrae, in honour of Lieutenant Alexis Helmer. A close friend of McCrae's, Helmer was killed by an enemy artillery shell in May 1915, during the fighting that continued after the Battle of Ypres.

Major John McCrae

Major John McCrae penned the now-famous lines of his poem, "In Flanders Fields," in May 1915, during the continuation of the Second Battle of Ypres. Born in 1872 and raised in Guelph, Ontario, McCrae was multi-talented: a physician, pathologist, writer and poet, he was educated at the University of Toronto, and later at McGill in Montreal. He wrote some of his first poems and short stories while still a medical student. McCrae also developed an early interest in military service; in high school he joined the cadet corps and, at age 15, served as a bugler in the local militia regiment of artillery commanded by his father. When the First World War erupted, McCrae had already served in the Boer War, and again volunteered his services to the military. In the fall of 1914, he was assigned as Brigade Surgeon to the First Brigade of Canadian Field Artillery.

Lieutenant-Colonel John McCrae and his dog, Bonneau. *Courtesy of the National Archives of Canada / C-046284.*

"In Flanders Fields" was written amid a horrifying loss of human life, confronted daily by McCrae in his duties as a surgeon on the Front Line. The poem was a tribute to the doctor's friend, Lieutenant Alexis Helmer, who was killed by an enemy artillery shell on May 2, 1915. It is believed that McCrae created the first draft of the famous verses on the night of Helmer's death. The following summer, the doctor was transferred to the Number 3 Canadian General Hospital in France, where he was placed second in command of medical services.

In January 1918, while carrying out his duties at the hospital, McCrae became ill with pneumonia – an illness that was complicated by his contracting meningitis shortly after. On January 24, while still ailing, McCrae was officially appointed as consulting physician to the First British Army – the first Canadian to receive this distinction. He died four days later, on January 28, 1918, and was buried with military honours at Wimereaux Cemetery in France.[12]

Following the battles at Ypres, the Canadians marched south from Belgium to join Allied offensives against the Germans at Festubert and Givenchy, villages in France. The fighting followed the war's grim pattern of frontal assault against powerful enemy positions defended by machine guns. Although the Canadians achieved their objectives, the territorial gains were almost negligible, while the cost in human lives was extremely high.

During the course of the war, Harry Colebourn received several medals and honours, including the 1914-1915 Star, British War Medal, 1914-1918, Victory Medal with Mentioned in Dispatches emblem[13] and the Colonial Auxiliary Forces Officer's Decoration awarded on November 26, 1928. Harry was also recognized for his services in the war by being recommended for the prestigious Order of the British Empire (OBE) by the Director of Canadian Veterinary Services, C.E. Edgett, DSO:

> For his untiring devotion to his duties as Veterinary Officer first with the Units in the Field, with whom he served for over three years, then as Senior Veterinary Officer of the Bramshott Area. This officer has always been most attentive to his professional charge and unsparing in his endeavors to produce efficiency, both when employed as an executive officer and as an administrative officer. He has been twice Mentioned in the Dispatches of the Field Marshal, Commander in Chief, British Forces in France, and was previously recommended by this department for an Honour.[14]

While Harry never did receive the OBE, his loyal services and tireless devotion to his veterinarian duties under formidable circumstances are a proud part of Canadian wartime history.

7: Winnie at the London Zoo

WHEN ON LEAVE from the war zones in France, Harry Colebourn would return to England and visit Winnie at the London Zoo as often as possible. Clearly, these meetings were important to him, all being carefully noted in his diary.

> July 8, 1915. In London all day. Visit Zoo in morning and see Winnie.
> July 12, 1915. 2 p.m. Went to Zoo. Saw Winnie.
> November 27, 1916. In London all day. Go to zoo with Grace and see Winnie. Have tea on Regent Street.[1]

It was also clear that Harry still intended to bring Winnie back home with him once the war was over. An undated note accompanied by a photograph that Colebourn sent to a friend during the war reads: "Myself and Winnie the Bear. Winnie is now on Exhibition at the Zoo in London but is coming back to Canada with me some day."[2]

The War Ends – Armistice, November 11, 1918

The term "armistice" essentially means a truce or a cessation of hostilities by common agreement of the opposing sides in a conflict. For the First World War, the Armistice refers to the agreement of November 11, 1918, between German and Allied forces that effectively ended the war.

Armistice negotiations began on October 4, 1918, and revolved around U.S. President Woodrow Wilson's "Fourteen Points," derived from a speech to Congress in which he outlined the conditions necessary for a just and lasting peace. While the Allies initially raised some concerns around the terms, negotiations ultimately led to a common understanding. The Supreme War Council at Versailles sent a draft of the agreement to Germany on November 5.

The Armistice was formally signed in the railway carriage of Allied Supreme Commander Ferdinand Foch, following the announcement of the abdication of the German Kaiser, Wilhelm II. Because the document was signed at 5 a.m., but actually came into effect at 11 a.m., it came to be that the war ended on the "eleventh hour of the eleventh day of the eleventh month."

Under the terms of the Armistice, the Germans had two weeks to withdraw from occupied territories on the Western Front. Germany was also required to abandon all other territories it occupied, as well as treaties it had negotiated with Romania and Russia. They were also warned that should they deviate in any way from the terms of the Armistice, that the Allied forces would resume hostilities within 48 hours. Until the Treaty of Versailles was signed the following year as a formal peace agreement, the armistice was regularly renewed, as it initially expired after a period of 36 days.

We honour Remembrance Day annually, in memory of those valiant men and women who contributed so much in the First World War, and in later world conflicts. Red poppies, symbolizing the sacrifice of so many, are worn in lapels and the words of John McCrae are recited and repeated across the land.

Harry, however, was to change his mind following his discharge from service after the war ended in 1918. By then, Winnie had become the star attraction at the zoo and virtually an institution in the minds of the citizens of London. Colebourn would have been quite aware of this and, no doubt, would have felt confident of the zoo's ability to provide appropriate care for Winnie. One can only assume he gave the matter much thought before making a momentous decision. On December 1, 1919,

Winnie standing at the London Zoo, circa 1916. *Courtesy of the Provincial Archives of Manitoba, Colebourn, D. Harry 16 Collection, No. N10474.*

Harry Colebourn officially donated Winnie to the London Zoo, an act that no doubt was appreciated by the thousands of people, young and old, who would visit this Canadian bear over her lifetime.

It was said that if Winnie had kept a visitor's book, it would have contained a surprising number of distinguished names. As she matured from a cub to a full-sized black bear, she remained good-natured and playful, winning over the hearts of all who encountered her. Completely gentle and trustworthy, Winnie gave immense pleasure to everyone, and no trouble to anyone. Clearly she was an extraordinary bear, but it was Harry's devotion and his gentleness with animals that would have contributed to shaping her behaviour with humans. It was even possible to take whatever she was eating away from her and she would simply accept it. Generally, it would be foolish to attempt to do this, even with a tame dog!

During wartime, the City of London was subjected to many air strikes.[3] At nighttime, the city was cloaked in darkness; buildings had blackout curtains to pull over the windows thus preventing light from escaping and creating a potential target for bombs. The sound of sirens was commonplace, warning people to seek shelter from an imminent attack. The strident noise from these air raid warnings caused the animals, including Winnie, to spend the hours of darkness in restlessness. They were greatly bothered by the hiss and patter of spent shrapnel, the fragments from an exploded bomb. However, despite the tensions, none of the animals escaped as all due care was taken to prevent such a disaster from occurring. A special emergency group of hand-picked staff was always within call, and precautions such as fitting heavy shutters to the glass fronts of the poisonous snakes' cages were followed every night.[4]

Winnie lived for nearly twenty years at the London Zoo, from 1914 through to 1934. She was described by zookeepers as the tamest bear that one could ever encounter and remained consistently so, even as she aged. Her unfailing, positive disposition was amazing; even the smallest child was safe with her. Harry Colebourn's son, Fred, remarked, "I'm sure that's because of the way my father treated her. He loved animals and they returned the affection."[5]

Several references to Winnie in books and newspapers about the animals at the London Zoo demonstrate her reliable good nature. It seems that in the 1920s, she was the darling of every child visitor to the Zoo. Even grown-ups clamoured to "stand Winnie a Winnie's cocktail"[6] – a quart tin filled with equal parts of condensed milk and golden syrup. She held this in both feet and forepaws and, astonishingly, would allow even a child to remove this from her when at the height of her enjoyment.

Jim Alldis, who worked at the London Zoo from 1927 to 1968, for a total of forty-one years, wrote a book about his experiences there, entitled *Animals as Friends: A Head Keeper Remembers the London Zoo*. In 1927, he simply had accepted a temporary job there, a "fill in" until he could decide what to make of his life. It was then that he met Winnie. His only interest in animals at that time was a fondness for farm horses and dogs, but the Canadian bear would contribute to his growing interest in the care of animals. In time, Mr. Alldis would work his way up to the position of Head Keeper. His first job, however, was at Regent Park, making tea and warming up the lunches for the workmen at the zoo. From his below level kitchen, he could see keepers passing back and forth carrying brooms, shovels and pails, obviously on their way to cleaning out the bear dens, which were situated on the terraces above his work area. In his book, he observed:

> Sometimes they [the keepers] took visitors to some mysterious spot; everyone was excited, especially the children, so I guessed this must have been a privilege and something very enjoyable.
>
> One day my curiosity got the better of me. I took the keepers a cup of tea and then wandered along the dark, gloomy passage leading to the sleeping quarters of the bears. I climbed a short wooden stairway, turned the corner – and found myself eyeball to eyeball with a full-grown Black Canadian Bear. My feet and legs went dead. If they'd had any life at all I would have been down those stairs and across the park in nothing flat, ending at speed my brief career at the Zoo; but I heard a voice say, "It's all right, she won't hurt you," and round the corner came the keeper.
>
> So I met Winnie the Pooh, hostess of so many At Homes [special events at the Zoo]. After that I often found time to go up and see her, taking with me some tinned condensed milk, for which she sat up and begged. When she had finished the milk, she would lie on

Winnie, featured in her own "signed" publicity shot, dated February 16, 1916. *Courtesy of the Provincial Archives of Manitoba, Colebourn, D. Harry 15 Collection, No. N10473.*

THE REAL WINNIE

her back and rock backwards and forwards as a way of saying thank you. I suppose Winnie was the reason for my deciding right then that this was my sort of thing. I had never really thought it possible that by kindness and patient training so much joy could be brought into the life of a creature in captivity. As I got to know the keepers better, I listened to their experiences with envy, for I could see they thought the world of Winnie.[7]

In her book *Behind the Scenes at the Zoo,* Helen Sidebotham writes about the bears at the London Zoo and describes Winnie as follows:

> Winnie, the tame bear, lives next to Young Sam and Barbara [polar bears]. She has been at the Zoo for ten years, and as she grows older she grows more and more gentle...If you go into her den she rubs against you like a dog, but although she is gentle she assumes that any paper bag you happen to be carrying is for her, and she will snatch at it the moment she catches sight of it. She likes oranges best, and in summer, when her friends are numerous, she will only accept a very rare and tempting offering. But in winter she will eat anything and is only too pleased to have a caller; her inclination is to hibernate, and the darkest corner of her den seems to attract her most.[8]

The *London Daily Express*, in 1931, describes Winnie as an older bear, seventeen years of age, quite an age for a black bear. At this time, her outer appearance was still quite youthful. Although she had lost her teeth, her coat was still beautiful and her ribs well covered. Evidently, she had retained her good nature. The *Express* described Winnie:

> Winsome Winnie, the dearest, tamest, most affectionate bear in the United Kingdom. Ask to see her – knock at the entrance to her suite, see her open the door herself to walk out. 'Do your daily dozen,' says her keeper. Winnie goes on her back and does her physical

Winnie with an unidentified woman at the London Zoo in the 1920s. *Courtesy of John Edwards, member of the Council of Trustees of the Zoological Society of London.*

THE REAL WINNIE

jerks. Feel her shoulders. She could crush you to death if she would. But not Winnie! A child can play with her.[9]

After finishing up the condensed milk the visitor had brought her, Winnie did some more exercises on her back, made her farewell, and retired with dignity to her apartment.

In another newspaper article dated September 27, 1933, Ernest Sceales, the London zookeeper who had been looking after the bears for ten years, warned people to never trust a bear completely, except for one:

> Only one bear at present in residence would I trust completely. That is Winnie, who is the original Winnie the Pooh. She is quite the tamest and best-behaved bear we have ever had at the Zoo.
>
> Winnie has never turned on anyone, and probably never will. She is so tame that the visitor who wants to make her acquaintance at close quarters can safely do so.
>
> Naturally so friendly an animal has made many human friends, and I expect Winnie has more human followers than any other Zoo star. Many though her admirers are, she never fails to recognize them, and she greets them all in the same doggish manner – by rubbing her big black flanks against their legs.[10]

It is apparent in reading these descriptions of various human encounters with Winnie, that she made a lasting impression on the people who saw her. Her visitors truly enjoyed the experience of her company and, clearly, she enjoyed their attention.

During Winnie's tenure, the London Zoo was a popular destination for the citizens of London, and people at the time were very involved and interested in the goings-on there. Reporters were always after a story from the zookeepers, especially about the "misbehaving" animals. Interestingly, few stories were written about Winnie in the general newspapers, in spite of her tremendous popularity; seemingly her gentle nature was not considered particularly newsworthy. In all her years at the London Zoo, never once did Winnie turn on anyone.

Winnie had several interesting neighbours on the Mappin Terraces. In one den there were three old female bears: Gypsy, Hector (who was named before she got to the Zoo and her sex properly determined) and Nellie. These three were nicknamed "The Three Bears" because of their curious habit of sitting upright in a row to beg for food. Even when they were almost blind, they never missed a bun thrown to them, swaying precariously about in order not to miss the catch, and always snatching the treat in mid-air. Apparently, Nellie even had a special trick she would perform; she would sit and hold her toes, rocking backwards and forwards until she was rewarded with a bun.[11]

Winnie's other neighbours on the Mappin Terraces were the polar bears, Sam and Barbara. Sam was known for his habit of snatching umbrellas from unwary visitors. It seems his aversion to umbrellas began when a visitor used an umbrella to poke him out of a sound sleep. Sam proceeded to capture the offending prod and demolish its silk and framework, losing his temper whenever he pricked his jaws on one of the steel spokes. From then on, Sam began collecting more umbrellas, and he invented an ingenious and rather ironic method of doing so; he would bait a "trap" and then rely on the good intentions of his unsuspecting human visitors. Sam, when fully extended, could stretch to a height of eleven feet. Almost that high above the floor of his enclosure there was a ledge and, on that ledge, he would place a piece of fresh fish. The shelf was easily within reach of those visitors outside the cage if they extended an umbrella or walking stick. Sam would crouch underneath, sniffing and whining piteously and pretending the fish was beyond his reach. As soon as a sympathetic individual reached down with an umbrella to push the piece of fish off the ledge and down to the waiting bear, Sam would extend to his full height, reach up and grab the umbrella with lightning speed, much to the chagrin of its well-intentioned owner. Sam kept his collection of mutilated umbrellas at the bottom of his pond, which the keeper cleared out from time to time.[12]

But no matter what tricks the other bears performed, none could come close to the popularity of their neighbour, Winnie. Little did anyone suspect that her fame was poised to extend well beyond the confines of the London Zoo.

8 : Enter Christopher Milne

IT WAS THE RENOWNED children's author A.A. Milne who catapulted Winnie's story into the minds and hearts of generations of children and parents, in the form of a loveable bumbling bear by the name of "Winnie the Pooh." Beginning in 1924, the writer took his young son, Christopher, to the London Zoo for a number of father-and-son visits. He was intrigued by the effect the zoo's special bear had on his four-year-old. Christopher declared Winnie to be his favourite animal in the whole of the zoo. The very young boy would spend time inside the bear's cage feeding condensed milk to a delighted Winnie. In his introduction to *Winnie the Pooh,* published in 1926, Milne describes the link to the White River bear:

> Christopher Robin once had a swan that he used to call Pooh. Well when Edward Bear said that he would like an exciting name all to himself, Christopher Robin said at once, without stopping to think, that he was Winnie-the-Pooh. And he was. So as I have explained the Pooh part, I will now explain the rest of it.
>
> When Christopher Robin goes to the Zoo, he goes to where the Polar Bears are, and he whispers something to the third keeper from the left, and the doors are unlocked and we wander through dark

passages and up steep stairs, until at last we come to the special cage, and the cage is opened, and out trots something brown and furry, and with a happy cry of "Oh, Bear!" Christopher Robin rushes into his arms. Now this bear's name is Winnie, which shows what a good name for bears it is.[1]

The imaginative young boy was so enthralled by Winnie that he named his much-loved teddy bear after her, adding the "Pooh" part in memory of his pet swan. The stuffed bear became a major part of Christopher's playtime, accompanying him to the Sussex countryside where the family vacationed. Whether he realized it or not, it appears that Milne began to keep a mental file of his son's adventures at the zoo and his make-believe with his own Pooh bear.

A.A. Milne

The author Alan A. Milne spent his childhood in London, England, where his father was a schoolmaster. His early education owed much to the skills of his young teacher and mentor, H.G. Wells. Years later, he described Wells as "a great writer and friend."[2] Milne continued his education at Westminster School and Trinity College, Cambridge, and worked as Assistant Editor at the magazine Punch *from 1906 to the outbreak of the First World War. In 1913, Alan Milne married Dorothy Daphne de Selincourt, and they had one son.*

Christopher was born to Alan and Daphne Milne on August 21, 1920. A year later he received a teddy bear for his first birthday. The bear had been purchased at Harrods. Probably it had been made in the factory of J.K. Farrell (established in 1897), the company making teddy bears exclusively for Harrods at this time.[3] Christopher's teddy bear seems to have gone under several other names (including Teddy, Edward, and Big Bear) before "Winnie" and "Pooh" were joined as a special name for it.

In December 1925, the author, already well-known for his collection of verse for children titled *When We Were Young*, was asked to write a story for the Christmas Eve issue of the *London Evening News*. His wife, Daphne, suggested that he write down one of the stories he was accustomed to telling to Christopher at bedtime. Most of these stories had been woven around "dragons and giants and magic rings," all designed to send a small boy, now nearly five-and-a-half, off to sleep. But there was one story that stood out, one that was true – the story about Christopher and his real bear, Winnie.

The tale that resulted was advertised on the front page of London's *Evening News*:

> A new story for children, "Winnie-the-Pooh," about Christopher Robin and his Teddy Bear, written by Mr. A.A. Milne specially for "The Evening News," appears tonight on Page Seven.
>
> It will be broadcast from all stations by Mr. Donald Calthrop, as part of the Christmas Day wireless programme, at 7:45 p.m. tomorrow.[4]

Milne's story was a lively, charming account of the exploits of a highly pragmatic little boy and a bear of strong opinion, but very little brain. It was a hit. Milne's fans loved the story, and new readers of all ages were drawn to it.

This most positive reception inspired Milne to go on to create an entire cast of characters around the boy and his bear. The work was published by Metheun as *Winnie the Pooh* in October of 1926. The staggering success of this book prompted him to write two more – the verses *Now We Are Six* and *The House At Pooh Corner* in 1928. The books soon became classics for children the world over and have remained firm favourites to this day. They were beautifully illustrated by Ernest H. Shepard, the man who became world-renowned as "the man who drew Pooh." Shepard's illustrations perfectly complemented Milne's text, and became works of art in their own right.

Despite the popularity of Winnie, it seemed to Alan Milne at the time that he should be writing something more serious, like a detective story, and even after the success of Pooh, he remained dubious about his creation. When he visited the United States in 1931, he acknowledged that it was his wife, Daphne, and his young son, Christopher, who inspired him to write the poems and stories about Winnie.

The main purpose of his trip was to publicize his adult novel, *Two People*, but it was Milne, the author of the children's books and father of Christopher Robin, in whom the Americans (and everybody else) were most interested. Even his detective story, *The Red House Mystery*, when it appeared as a paperback, carried the telling addition, "By the author of *Winnie-the-Pooh*."[5]

White River, Ontario, has reclaimed the origins of Winnie. A large sculpture by George Barone of Kelowna, BC, stands near the Visitors Centre overlooking the Trans-Canada Highway. It was unveiled in 1992. Fred Colebourn was part of the large crowd attracted to the event. Today the statue of Winnie the Pooh with his treasured honey pot reaches out to all who come by. *Courtesy of the Township of White River.*

Daphne Milne, Christopher's mother, travelled to America with her husband in 1931. While there, she was interviewed for *Parents Magazine*. In the article she expressed her views on the differences between American and English children. She saw American children as being much more mature than their English counterparts, due to differences in their background and environment. English children kept to the nursery and were less exposed to adult conversation and concerns, thus inhabiting a little world all to themselves. Not surprisingly then, English children, in her opinion, stayed very simple and young. Daphne observed, "life is more stimulating in your large cities. There is so much provided for children to do. They go to matinees, operettas, and moving picture performances. Few amusements of this sort exist for English children to attend. Theirs is a very quiet, unexciting existence with walks in the park to feed the squirrels and occasional visits to the zoo their most thrilling diversions."[6] It was Daphne who confirmed that Christopher had named his bear after Winnie at the London Zoo:

> Incidentally, Christopher named his bear for the famous big brown
> one at the London Zoo, dear to the hearts of innumerable children.[7]

From her humble origins as an orphaned black bear cub from the White River area of Northern Ontario, Winnie had become the most famous bear in the world.

9 : The Closing Years

CAPTAIN HARRY COLEBOURN survived The Great War although he had at least one close call. Fred Colebourn, his son, remembered asking how his father had acquired the white scar on the top of his head. His father explained that it was from a sniper bullet which had penetrated his steel helmet while he was working close to the battle trenches in France.[1] Following the end of the war, Harry Colebourn remained in England for a short while to further his veterinary education and training by enrolling in a post-graduate course at the Royal College of Veterinary Surgeons in London. Upon graduation from that institution, he was accorded the title of Member of the Royal College of Veterinary Surgeons (MRCVS). During that period of time, Harry would continue to see Winnie, but only as a visitor to the zoo, albeit one with great love for Winnie and her antics.

It was not until early 1920 that Harry returned to Winnipeg. Rather than immediately resuming his former position with the Department of Agriculture, he chose to open a private veterinary practice on McMillan Avenue. There he treated mostly horses, as well as a range of small animals. This, however, was a period of great change in his life. In 1923, Harry married Christina McLeod and their only child, Fred, was born on March 10, 1925.

During that same period, Winnipeg began to experience economic stagnation due to a combination of sustained drought and low wheat prices. The depressed economy was to last for some time. In 1926, Harry gave up his private practice to accept a position with his earlier employer, the Health of Animals Branch in the Department of Agriculture, as a veterinarian specializing in post-mortem work. It seems as if the need to ensure a steady income for his family was foremost in his mind. However, that may not have been the only impetus for Colebourn to leave full-time private practice. At the time, Colebourn viewed the future of veterinary medicine with pessimism, for he spoke of it as a "dying profession" and did not encourage his son to follow in his footsteps.[2] The mechanization of all forms of transport and delivery services in Winnipeg had escalated over a few short years. Horses – and hence the services of the veterinarians who cared for them – were needed less and less. In spite of this, however, Colebourn was content with the career path he had chosen. Fortunately, Harry's fear did not materialize, and the recreational use of horses has had a resurgence in popularity. Veterinarians are still much in demand.

Harry Colebourn maintained his relationship with The Fort Garry Horse and remained as their Veterinary Officer with the rank of Major from January 15, 1921, until his retirement from the military on April 15, 1929.[3]

For a number of years after Harry's departure from London, Winnie continued to delight her many fans, in spite of her advancing years. Around 1931, her health began to fail and the zoo authorities retired her from the public eye. She was kept in a special apartment at the back of the Mappin Terraces, but continued to receive privileged visitors.

Even though she had cataracts in both eyes and was all but blind, as well as suffering from osteoarthritis,[4] she never lost her love for human companionship. Although she refused to take any medicine – no matter how it was disguised – Winnie would help her keeper look after her. Before lying down, she would wrap her feet up in blankets to ease her aching joints.[5] In the last two years of her life, a stroke left her partly paralyzed and her health deteriorated further, but she continued to eat regularly.[6] On May 12, 1934, at the age of 20, Winnie was euthanized. The Record Card kept at the London Zoo reads:

K.B.O. [Killed By Order]. Senile Debility. Cataract of both eyes.
Osteoarthritis. 12.5.34.

She was the original "Winnie the Pooh" from whom A.A. Milne
got the name for his son's Teddy Bear.[7]

At the time of Winnie's death, Harry Colebourn was still working with the
Department of Agriculture in Winnipeg; he did so for over twenty-one years. Right
up to his retirement on May 19, 1945, he also maintained a part-time private practice
in conjunction with a small animal hospital he had built at the rear of his family
home, at 600 Corydon Avenue. There, he dedicated many hours of both paid and
unpaid service to numerous animals and their owners; he would not turn an animal
away because its owner could not pay.

Harry's love of and dedication to animals remained the driving force behind his
life until September 24, 1947. On that day, at sixty years of age, he did not recover
from a fall down the basement stairs of his home. It appears that he may have had a
heart attack.[8] Major Harry Colebourn is buried in Brookside Cemetery, Winnipeg,
in the Field of Honour. Fred Colebourn, Harry's only son, passed away in March
1998, in Winnipeg.[9]

At the time of his death, Harry Colebourn was unaware of the tremendous international fame that had come to his one-time charge, Winnie. According to Fred
Colebourn, they both were well aware of A.A. Milne's books and certainly knew
that Pooh Bear was based on Winnie, but they simply did not realize the scope of the
popularity.[10] It was his son, Fred, who in his later years helped to publicize his father's
association with the bear in several newspaper and journal articles, and through radio
interviews. Today the story is celebrated across Canada, especially in White River and
Winnipeg.

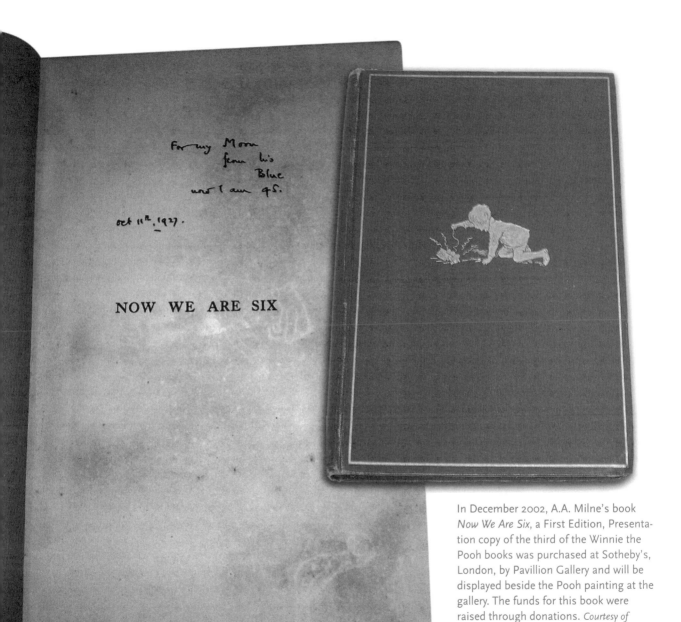

For my Moon
from his
Blue
until I am 45.

oct 11ᵗʰ, 1927.

NOW WE ARE SIX

In December 2002, A.A. Milne's book *Now We Are Six*, a First Edition, Presentation copy of the third of the Winnie the Pooh books was purchased at Sotheby's, London, by Pavillion Gallery and will be displayed beside the Pooh painting at the gallery. The funds for this book were raised through donations. *Courtesy of Partners in the Park Museum.*

10: The Legacy of Winnie

TODAY, THE TREMENDOUS popularity of the bear Winnie is known around the world. Although A.A. Milne's stories introducing Winnie the Pooh are over seventy-five years old, they remain classics in the world of children's literature. The four Pooh books have sold more than fifty million copies in some thirty-three languages around the world. In 1961, the Walt Disney Company acquired the rights to "Winnie the Pooh."[1] Disney's feature-length animated film that followed was an immense success and, by 1996, Pooh Bear had become one of the most popular of all the Disney characters.

Amazingly, the story of the real Winnie's origins remained buried, likely not even queried, for years. It was not until 1987 that the story made its way to public attention. Seemingly a newspaper in Calgary published an account, but attributed the donation of the bear to the London Zoo to a Canadian regiment other than Harry Colebourn's.[2] Fred Colebourn, living in Winnipeg, decided to correct the error publicly. That decision led to a radio interview, and the link with White River was broadcast to a wider audience. The Canadian Winnie was revealed at last.

Today, White River, Winnipeg and the London Zoo are all proud of their connections with Harry Colebourn and Winnie. White River, Ontario, considers itself Winnie's birthplace and hometown; Winnipeg, the original name for the bear, was also home to Harry Colebourn; and Winnie made her home on the Mappin Terraces at the London Zoo for twenty years. All are part of Winnie's history and all have stories to celebrate.

White River, Ontario

The town of White River, Ontario, with a population of about 1,200 people, is some 280 kilometres (168 miles) northwest of Sault Ste. Marie. A resilient community, the town shifted from its origins as a railway town to a thriving lumber town in the 1920s. Many residents, by the 1980s, were employed by Domtar Forest Products, which operated a state-of-the-art sawmill located just outside of town. When the Trans-Canada Highway (Highway 17) was completed in 1970, running through White River on the route to Thunder Bay, it created the potential of a whole new industry – tourism. White River has responded to the opportunity in a variety of ways. One totally unexpected promotional prospect came their way with Fred Colebourn's broadcasted interview in 1987. White River had a whole new story to tell the world.

By 1988, Fred's assertions had been verified by a battery of researchers.[3] A dedicated community group made the initial contact with Fred and invited him to White River and the site of his father's historic purchase of the bear he first called Winnipeg. The excitement generated led to many such visits and, ultimately, to Fred Colebourn's role as guest of honour at the first annual Winnie Hometown Festival in 1989 – the 75th anniversary of Harry Colebourn's initial meeting with Winnie.[4] The White River Historical Society, credited as the founders of the annual festival, next took on the task of creating a museum. In the year 2000, the White River Heritage Museum opened, and today takes great pride in displaying not only historical artifacts of the community, but also an extensive collection of Winnie the Pooh items and related merchandise.

Officials of the Township of White River, working with the local Chamber of Commerce, were determined to erect a giant Winnie the Pooh statue, right beside the Trans-Canada Highway – a place of honour for their most famous offspring. Initially, however, permission to use the cartoon image was rebuffed by the Walt Disney Company. Although public pressure may have played a role in the altering of their decision, in 1991 the corporation relented, declaring that their contractual obligations would

The exterior of the White River Heritage Museum. Opened in 2000, the museum features the heritage of White River and Winnie memorabilia. *Courtesy of the White River Heritage Museum.*

not be violated in this instance, but the statue would have to resemble Ernest Shepard's drawings, not the Disney character.[5] The local officials agreed, and Winnie would come home. The project attracted enormous international attention and White River was now on the media map.

An article in *The Daily Telegraph* on September 12, 1989, written by Jonathan Petre in New York, described plans for the building of the Winnie statue in White River:

> The statue's plinth will be eight feet (2.4 metres) high to allow it to appear over the snow line during the long winters and, of course, to keep Pooh's toes from growing too cold.
>
> The 25-foot (7.6 metre) statue will stand on the corner of the town's high street and the Trans-Canada highway.

Italian-born George Barone, of Kelowna, BC, with the reputation of being Canada's foremost community sculptor, was selected as the artist to create the statue.

An interior shot of the museum display of Winnie the Pooh memorabilia. Through a licensed agreement with the Walt Disney Company, a line of products is available with the "Where It All Began" logo. *Courtesy of the White River Heritage Museum.* *Logo courtesy of the Township of White River.*

His completed structure, made of marbelite and based on a design provided through Walt Disney Co. (Canada) Ltd., was unveiled on August 22, 1992, two days before Winnie's 78th birthday.[6] Fred Colebourn attended the official occasion as did the statue designers, Anthony Van Bruggen and Alvaro Cervantes from the United States. Master of ceremonies for the day was White River economic development manager Norm Jaehrling, who welcomed the crowd of almost 1,000. Today, the Winnie the Pooh statue commands the attention of all who venture by the White River Tourist Information Centre. Inside the centre, a plaque – the duplicate of the one that the Grade Eight class from St. Basil's School took to England and presented to the Zoo – is on display. There is also a cedar chainsaw carving of Captain Colebourn and Winnie by artist Orville Mowers, which was unveiled at the first festival in 1989. Winnie's birthplace, her London home and the legacy of A.A. Milne's character are linked in perpetuity.

Winnipeg, Manitoba

It is quite likely that A.A. Milne did not know that Christopher's favourite bear in the London Zoo was named after the City of Winnipeg. And as noted, it is only relatively recently that this astounding link between Winnie the Pooh and the city has become public knowledge, even in Winnipeg itself. The Manitoba city has grown steadily since Harry Colebourn's time there. Positioned as a major grain, financial, manufacturing and transportation centre in Western Canada, the city's current population is over 680,000. Winnipeg, with its robust cultural life and a heritage enriched by immigrants from around the world, is proud of its connection to Harry and to Winnie.

Within the city's Assiniboine Park Zoo is an almost life-size bronze statue of the veterinary officer and his bear. Created by the late sculptor William Epp in 1992, the sculpture depicts Lieutenant Harry Colebourn in full military uniform holding the forepaws of a standing, cub-sized Winnie, each ostensibly focusing attention on the other. The adjacent plaque reads:

> On August 24, 1914, while en route overseas during World War I, Lieutenant Harry Colebourn of The 34th Fort Garry Horse Regiment of Manitoba purchased a black Canadian bear cub at White River, Ontario. He named her Winnie after Winnipeg, his hometown. The bear became the pet of the soldiers. While Lieutenant Colebourn served in France, she was left in the care of the London Zoo. In 1919, he gave her to the Zoo where she was visited and loved by many, including the author A.A. Milne and his son Christopher.
>
> In 1926, A.A. Milne gave the fictional character Winnie-the-Pooh, named after Lieutenant Colebourn's bear, to Christopher Robin and his friends for posterity. Winnie died at the London Zoo on May 12, 1934.

The tradition of the famous Canadian bear lives on in many forms. On September 20, 1997, during a ceremony to reaffirm and permit The Fort Garry Horse to exercise

The near life-sized
statue in Winnipeg's
Assiniboine Park
Zoo is based on
the 1914 photograph
of Captain Harry
Colebourn and his
bear cub Winnie.
The statue, by
Saskatoon sculptor
William Epp,
was unveiled on
August 6, 1992.
*Courtesy of Val
Shushkewich.*

The Pavilion, situated in beautiful Assiniboine Park in Winnipeg, Manitoba, was built in 1908. It was destroyed by fire in 1929. The second Pavilion, designed by local architectural firm, Northwood and Chivers, officially opened on May 24, 1930. After 70 years as a prominent, but underutilized structure, The Pavilion was beautifully restored and renovated to reflect its rich, distinguished history and style. Re-opened in 1998, it features three galleries showcasing the works of Ivan Eyre, Walter J. Phillips and Clarence Tillenius. There is a Gift Shop on the Main Floor and the Tavern in the Park, a garden restaurant situated in a glass-roof atrium. Photo by Alan McTavish. *Courtesy of Partners in the Park Museum.*

their traditional right of the "Freedom of the City," the Assiniboine Park Zoo's eighteen–month old black bear (called Winnie after the first Winnie the Bear) was named as the regiment's mascot.

The significance of Winnie to Winnipeg took on a whole new dimension on November 16, 2000. The Pavilion Gallery Museum, located in Assiniboine Park, paid 124,250 British pounds (then the equivalent of $300,000 in Canadian dollars) for the only known oil painting of Winnie the Pooh by Ernest H. Shepard, the illustrator of Milne's Pooh books. Hartley T. Richardson, a descendant of one of the best-known and most influential families in Winnipeg, along with the City of Winnipeg, the federal government, the Canadian Cultural Board and many, many citizens of the city, provided help and encouragement in raising the funds. This painting, officially titled *Winnie the Pooh and the Honey Pot*, was originally created in the 1930s. In his remarks on June 3, 2001, at the official welcoming ceremony to unveil the painting of the famous bear with his honey pot, the Lieutenant Governor of Manitoba, the Honourable Peter M. Liba, captured the spirit of the ceremony as he uttered these words: "Honey never tasted as sweet as this Manitoba moment!"[8]

The unique and binding connection between Winnipeg and Winnie continues to gather momentum. "Partners in the Park," a non-profit group of volunteers, along with other philanthropic interests, have raised millions of dollars for other creative ventures. After acquiring Shepard's painting, Partners in the Park has continued to raise funds and collect Winnie memorabilia. In August 2003, the Winnipeg art dealer David Loch, who was instrumental in the acquisition of Shepard's painting, took delivery of a rare copy of A.A. Milne's *Now We Are Six*. Purchased at an auction the previous winter for almost $100,000, this collectible is inscribed by Milne as a gift to his son, Christopher.

Plans are to develop the northwest corner of Assiniboine Park to celebrate the Winnie legacy with a "Poohseum," to be built next to the Pavilion. There is to be room for an adjacent "Hundred-Acre Woods" development where children can go on "expotitions," as Milne would say.

With the United Nations having designated Winnie the Pooh as a "friendship" ambassador to the children of the world, Winnipeg can be viewed as a centre for international friendship.

Mappin Terraces, London Zoo

Throughout its long life, the London Zoo and its owner, the Zoological Society of London, have always had to adapt in order to survive. In the late 1980s, the zoo experienced severe financial jeopardy and was in danger of closure. Today, although still a popular attraction for the visiting public, the zoo emphasizes its involvement with serious animal rearing and research programs (which it has always had since its inception, and long before it was fashionable or essential). Of the more than 650 species presently at the London Zoo, 112 are listed as threatened; the breeding program involves 130 different species.

The painting, *Winnie the Pooh and the Honey Pot*, is the only known oil painting of Winnie the Pooh created by the artist Ernest H. Shepard. It originally hung above the door of a teashop in Bristol, England, called "Pooh Corner" for ten years, and was offered for sale at Sotheby's, London, in November 2000. A group of interested citizens from Winnipeg launched a fundraising campaign and was successful in acquiring the painting. It is now on display at the Pavilion Gallery. Photograph by Ernest Mayer. *Courtesy of Partners in the Park Museum.*

The London Zoo recognizes Winnie as one of the most famous animals ever to live there and the Mappin Terraces is still acknowledged as one of the most magnificent naturalistic zoo structures in the world. It was there that Christopher Milne unveiled a three-and-a-half foot bronze replica of Winnie the Bear, by sculptor Lorne McKean, in 1981. Part of the inscription on the plaque reads:

> She gave her name to Winnie the Pooh and A.A. Milne and Ernest
> Shepard gave Winnie the Pooh to the rest of the world.

The plaque presented to the zoo in 1997 by the St. Basil's Grade 8 Class from White River detailing their community's role in Winnie's story is on view, and establishes her early history for zoo visitors. Two years later, in 1999, a party of officers and men from The Fort Garry Horse in Winnipeg visited the London Zoo and unveiled a new plaque established at the Mappin Terraces, dedicated to Harry Colebourn and Winnie:

> Major Harry Colebourn M.R.C.V.S.
> 34th Fort Garry Horse and Canadian Army Veterinary Corps
>
> Original donor of the bear "Winnie" to the London Zoo, December 1914
>
> Lieutenant Colebourn was the first Veterinary Officer of The 34th Fort Garry Horse when the Regiment was formed in Winnipeg in 1912. Upon the declaration of war in August 1914, he transferred to the Canadian Army Veterinary Corps, and was attached to the 2nd and 4th Canadian Infantry Brigades in France. He served there until the end of the war, being promoted to the rank of Captain. Back in Winnipeg, he re-joined The Fort Garry Horse in 1921 as a Major and continued to serve until his retirement from the Militia in 1929. A successful veterinary surgeon in civilian life, he continued to serve the needs of animals until his death in 1947.

Sponsored by the Province of Manitoba
Presented by the members, past and present
The Fort Garry Horse
Winnipeg, Manitoba, Canada
30 May 1999

The story of the real Winnie, once known only to a select few, has captured the imagination of many. From a relatively obscure beginning in Northern Ontario to international fame that continues into the twenty-first century, Winnie has become an icon for Canada.

Conclusion

IN REFLECTING UPON the lives of both Harry Colebourn and Winnie, it is interesting to note the inherent qualities apparent in both the man and his bear. Both were extraordinarily kind, gentle and generous throughout their lives. Possibly Harry Colebourn, with his sensitivity to animals, recognized Winnie's sweet disposition and endearing ways when he first laid eyes on her on the train station platform at White River. Their special relationship is immortalized in the bronze statue in Assiniboine Park Zoo in Winnipeg.

But Winnie's legacy is a living one; her reach extends beyond plaques and monuments, beyond bronze and stone. The true story of this real bear – who faced life in an open, honest way, who never lost her temper or snapped at anyone – should be seen as just that: a true story, a real-life example of the potential goodness that lives in the hearts of humans and animals, which promotes love and respect and inspires imagination. This chain of goodness, set against dark moments in world history and put in motion by one kind-hearted young soldier who rescued an orphan bear, has not been broken. Immortalized by A.A. Milne, Winnie has linked together generations, both young and old, in their delight at seeing the story of one sweet, gentle and bumbling bear told time and time again – now and for countless years to come.

Introduction

1.   It is estimated that a total of ten million lives were lost, according to *the Canadian Oxford Dictionary*, Oxford University Press Canada, 1998.

Chapter 1: The Stage Is Set

1.   Courtesy of newspaper article "Little did Colebourn know ...", obtained from the White River District Historical Society, White River, Ontario.

2.   Physical description taken from Attestation Paper (for Harry Colebourn), Canadian Overseas Expeditionary Force, signed by Harry Colebourn, September 25, 1914. National Archives of Canada, Harry Colebourn service record, RG 150, acc. 92-93/166, box 1844.

3.   From "Lt. Harry Colebourn and Winnie-the-Bear," original biographical sketch written by Harry Colebourn's son, the late Fred Colebourn, in May 1988. Subsequently edited and corrected by CWO Gordon Crossley, Fort Garry Horse Museum and Archives, May 1999/August 2000. http://www.fortgarryhorse.ca/HTML/winnie-the-bear.html, accessed Jan. 26, 2003. © 2002 – The Fort Garry Horse Museum and Archives.

4.   Ontario Veterinary College (OVC): Harry Colebourn was part of the first class to graduate with a three-year Bachelor of Veterinary Science degree from OVC, in affiliation with the University of Toronto, a union that was established in 1897. The college relocated to Guelph in 1922 and became part of the University of Guelph in 1964.

5.   Adapted from the Dictionary of Canada Biography Online, www.biographi.ca, October 2003.

Chapter 2: At the White River Railway Station

1.   Information on White River, an article "White River" provided by Terry Delaney of the White River Heritage Museum, received October 2003.

2.   Mary Houston, *White River – 100 Years, Pictorial History* (White River, ON: privately published, 1985) 15.

3.   *Ibid,* 45.

4.   From the diaries of Harry Colebourn, Colebourn Collection, on microfilm at the Provincial Archives of Manitoba.

5.   "Little did Colebourn know ...," from the White River District Historical Society, White River, Ontario.

6.   Background on bears from Rebecca Stefoff, *Bears.* New York: Benchmark Books, Marshall Cavendish, 2002.

7.   *Ibid.*

Chapter 3: En Route to England

1.   Information taken from Cecil French (C.A.V. Barker and Ian K. Barker, eds.), *A History of the Canadian Army Veterinary Corps in the Great World War 1914-1918* (Guelph, ON: Crest Books, 1999) 5.

2.   Information on Valcartier Camp taken from http://www.rootsweb.com/~cansk/CanadaInFlanders/ChapterI.html, accessed May 30, 2003.

3.   Canadian Great War Homepage, part of the Canadian Military Heritage Project, www.rootsweb.com/~wwican/, October 2003.

4.   French (Barker and Barker, eds.) 5.

5.   Jennifer Grainger, *Vanished Villages of Middlesex* (Toronto: Natural Heritage Books, 2002) 13-14.

6.   French (Barker and Barker, eds.) 5.

7.   From the diaries of Harry Colebourn.

8. Information taken from the Statement of the Service of Major Harry Colebourn, November 26, 1928; this document is attached to his CEF service record, National Archives of Canada, RG150, acc. 92-93/166, box 1844.

9. French (Barker and Barker, eds.) 5, 252.

10. *Ibid*, 5, 252.

11. Taken from "Troop Convoy – How Canada Went to War in 1914, in Crowsnest," published in October, 1964. The article summarizes the speech given by Rear-Admiral Hugh Pullen, RCN, on Oct. 10, 1964 to the Red Chevron Club of Ottawa (many of their members were those who had gone overseas with the First Contingent – 32,000 men – of the Canadian Expeditionary Force in October, 1914). http://www.gwpda.org/naval/1cdncvy.htm, accessed March 28, 2002.

12. *Ibid*.

13. The term Allies refers to the nations allied against the Central Powers in the First World War (1914-1918), primarily the British Commonwealth (including Canada), France, the Russian Empire, and later the United States.

14. Anthony Preston, *Submarine Warfare: An Illustrated History* (San Diego, Thunder Bay Press, 1999).

15. From the diaries of Harry Colebourn.

Chapter 4: On the Salisbury Plain

1. A reference to imprinting is found in the notes section of Cecil French's (Barker and Barker eds.) *A History of the Canadian Army Veterinary Corps in the Great World War 1914-1919* (Guelph, ON: Crest Books, 1999) 253. According to Encyclopedia Britannica online, in psychobiology, imprinting is considered a form of learning in which a very young animal fixes its attention on the very first object with which it has visual, auditory or tactile experience and thereafter follows that object. In nature, the object is almost invariably a parent, but in experiments, other animals and even inanimate objects have been successfully substituted.

2. From the diaries of Harry Colebourn.

Chapter 5: First Days at the London Zoo

1.   From the web site http://library.thinkquest.org/12405/raffles.htm, October 2003.

2.   "Alfred Peck Stevens. a popular English actor in the mid-1800s who billed himself as "The Great Vance," is credited with coining the word "zoo." In 1870, his song "Walking in the Zoo" was all the rage, much to the consternation of the Fellows of Royal Society who attempted, without success, to insist on the full title, Royal Zoological Society's Gardens. From http://www.peopleplayuk.org.uk/collections/object.php?search_result=true&object_id=577, October 2003.

3.   From the web site of the Zoological Society of London on the architectural history of the London Zoo. http://www.londonzoo.co.uk/history/architecture.html, accessed on March 24, 2003.

4.   "Moving the Animals," *The Guardian Unlimited*, Tuesday, May 26, 1914.

5.   "Mascots at the Gardens," in *The Field*, a publication of the Zoological Society of London, 1915.

Chapter 6: To the Battlefields

1.   From the diaries of Harry Colebourn.

2.   From the journal article by D.T. Ladry, "Winnie the Pooh and the Veterinarian Too: A Biographical Essay on the Life of Dr. Harry Colebourn, VBSc, MRCVS (1887-1947)," in *Veterinary Heritage*, bulletin of the American Veterinary History Society, Vol. 21, No. 2, December 1998.

3.   From an account by Nick Balmer of his grandfather's reminiscences as a Veterinary Officer in the British Army throughout the First World War, accessed from http://members.lycos.co.uk/blewholt/wwihorsedespatch/page6.html, on May 30, 2003.

4.   *Report of the Ministry, Overseas Military Forces of Canada 1918*, (London: Printed by Authority of the Ministry, Overseas Military Forces of Canada) 268.

5. *Ibid*, 269.

6. Extract from the *Official Field Service Pocket Book of 1914*, issued by H.M. Stationery Office, price One Shilling. Source is from "Veterinary Service, including simple advice and treatment in the field," on http://www.ku.edu/carrie/specoll/medical/vetindex.htm, accessed on May 30, 2003.

7. The Battle of the Somme on the Western Front in northern France (July to November 1916), between British-led forces (including Canadians) and the Germans, cost more than a million casualties on both sides.

8. No Man's Land is the name given to the so-called "dead space" between warring armies; in the context of The Great War (1914-18), it refers to the gulf between the Allied and German trenches. The outer limits of this wasteland – filled with craters created by exploding shells, blackened tree stumps and rotting corpses – could change rapidly as front lines shifted. Cordoned off by barbed wire, the area of No Man's Land was most static along the trenches of the Western Front, but its width varied. Some places the distance between enemy troops was only a few hundred metres (or yards), but the space could be up to one kilometre (0.6 mile) wide.

9. According to Richard Feltoe, Curator of the Redpath Museum, the first Canadian officer killed in action in The Great War was Guy Drummond, grandson of John Redpath, the founder of Redpath Sugar, and son of George Alexander Drummond, Canadian Senator and Vice President of the Bank of Montreal.

10. Every effort has been made to locate the credit for this visual, which appeared in the article by Ted Weatherhead, "In Which Pooh Joins the Army and Lands in the Zoo," in the October/November 1989 issue of *The Beaver*.

11. The battle took place near Ypres, a town in Belgium, along the border with France.

12. Adapted from "The Story of John McCrae" by John Peddie, at www.museum.guelph.on.ca/mccraejohn.htm, October 2003.

13. M.I.D. (Mentioned in Dispatches) London Gazette #30107, June 1, 1917.

14. "Lt. Harry Colebourn and Winnie-the-Bear," biographical sketch.

Chapter 7: Winnie at the London Zoo

1.   Excerpt from the diaries of Harry Colebourn.

2.   Information is in the file of the Provincial Archives of Manitoba, Colebourn, D. Harry Collection, N10467.

3.   The first German air attacks against Britain were carried out with Zeppelin airships, beginning in December 1914. In May 1917, the task was given over to aircraft. The strikes led to the loss of civilian lives and extensive damage to England's cities. As the bombers did not have the technology to provide the accuracy necessary to aim for and hit strategic targets like military installations, the location of potential air strikes was unpredictable. Whole cities, including London, remained blacked out at night to avoid detection from the air.

4.   L.R. Brightwell, "The Zoo Revolution 1911-1920," in *The Zoo You Knew?* (Oxford: Basil Blackwell, 1936) 198.

5.   "Pooh Bear's name is Winnie as in Winnipeg" by Heidi Graham, in the *Winnipeg Free Press*, May 2, 1987.

6.   Brightwell, 199.

7.   Jim Alldis, *Animals As Friends, A Head Keeper Remembers London Zoo* (New York: London Zoo, Taplinger Publishing Co. Inc., 1973) 9.

8.   Helen Sidebotham, *Behind the Scenes at the Zoo* (London: Cassel and Company, Ltd., 1925) 34.

9.   Ted Weatherhead "In Which Pooh joins the Army and lands in the Zoo," *The Beaver, Exploring Canada's History, 75th Anniversary Special Issue*, October/November 1989.

10.   "A Bear That Catches Pigeons," *London Daily Express*, Sept. 27, 1933.

11.   Sidebotham, 35.

12.   Leslie G. Mainland *Secrets of the Zoo* (London: S.W. Partridge & Co., Ltd., 1923) 55. ("L.G.M." of *The Daily Mail*.)

Chapter 8: Enter Christopher Milne

1. From http://www.geocities.com/lovanne°wendy/poohhist.html, accessed October 21, 2003. Taken from the "Introduction" to *Winnie-the-Pooh* by A.A. Milne, illustrated by E.H. Shepard: Copyright under the Berne Convention; in Canada copyright 1926 by E.P. Dutton, renewed copyright 1954 by A.A. Milne.

2. From http://www.pooh-corner.com/biomilne.html, official web site of Peter Dennis, who does audio recordings and live performances of the "Winnie the Pooh" stories.

3. Anne Thwaite, *The Brilliant Career of Winnie-the-Pooh: The story of A.A. Milne and his writing for children* (London: Methuen, 1992) 36.

4. *Ibid,* 76.

5. *Ibid,* 132.

6. "Now We Are Eleven," by Mrs. A.A. Milne, as told to Sara J. Wardel, *Parents Magazine,* April 1931.

7. *Ibid.*

Chapter 9: The Closing Years

1. D.T. Ladry, "Winnie the Pooh and the Veterinarian Too: A Biographical Essay on the Life of Dr. Harry Colebourn, VBSc, MRCVS (1887-1947)," in *Veterinary Heritage,* (bulletin of the American Veterinary History Society), Vol. 21, No. 2, December 1998.

2. *Ibid.*

3. Fred Colebourn, "Lt. Harry Colebourn and Winnie-the-Pooh."

4. Osteoarthritis is a degenerative disease of the cartilage in joints that causes pain and stiffness of movement, mostly found in those middle-aged and older.

5. "Winnie, Noted Canadian Black Bear Who Amused Londoners at Zoo Passes," *Winnipeg Free Press,* July 13, 1934.

6. *Ibid.*

7. From a copy of Winnie's Record Card that was kept at the London Zoo, www.pooh-corner.com, October 2003.

8. From a telephone conversation with Lindsay Mattick, great-granddaughter of Harry Colebourn, October 29, 2003.

9. Fred Colebourn made Winnipeg his home throughout his life. He and his wife, Ella, had three daughters, Laureen, Wendy and Brenda.

10. Ted Weatherhead, "In Which Pooh joins the Army and lands in the Zoo," *The Beaver* 75th Anniversary, October/November, 1989, 38.

Chapter 10: The Legacy of Winnie

1. *Ontario Report*, published by Ontario House, New York, Winter 1993.

2. "Winnie the Pooh home at last," by Valerie Wilson (only identified as "of our North Bay Bureau"). From newspaper clippings, courtesy of the Township of White River.

3. "Who would believe that 'silly old bear' came from Canada?" by Marjie Smith, *The Star*, clipping not dated, and "Creation of Winnie-the-Pooh traced to bear," attributed to Winnipeg (CP), from newspaper clippings, courtesy of the Township of White River.

4. Information on the discovery of Winnie's origins and the initiation of Winnie's Hometown Festival is from print material produced by the White River Heritage Museum.

5. "Pooh's hometown can put up his statue" by Vicky Vaughan of the *Sentinel* staff. From newspaper clippings provided by the Township of White River.

6. Information on the Winnie the Pooh statue taken from print material provided by the Township of White River.

7. In the early 1960s, the City of Winnipeg was twinned with Setagaka-ku, part of the City of Tokyo. Kensen Saito, now a Canadian citizen, can still remember when Prime Minister

John Diefenbaker visited his elementary school as part of the twinning ceremony. He and his classmates had made a totem pole to honour the occasion.

8.   From http://lg.gov.mb.ca/speech/2001/mayjun/winniethepooh.html, October 2003

Bibliography

A. Articles

Colebourn, Fred, "Lt. Harry Colebourn and Winnie-the-Bear," original biographical sketch written by Harry Colebourn's son, the late Fred Colebourn, in May 1988. Subsequently edited and corrected by CWO Gordon Crossley, Fort Garry Horse Museum and Archives, May 1999/August 2000. http://www.fortgarryhorse.ca/HTML/winnie-the-bear.html, accessed January 26th, 2003. © 2002 – The Fort Garry Horse Museum and Archives.

Graham, Heidi, "Pooh Bear's Name Is Winnie," *Winnipeg Free Press*, May 2, 1987.

Ladry, D.T., "Winnie the Pooh and the Veterinarian Too: A Biographical Essay on the Life of Dr. Harry Colebourn, VBSc, MRCVS (1887-1947)," in *Veterinary Heritage*, bulletin of the American Veterinary History Society, Vol. 21, No. 2, December 1998.

"Mascots at the Gardens" in *The Field*, a publication of the Royal Zoological Society of London, 1915.

Milne, Mrs. A.A. (as told to Sara J. Wardel), *Parents Magazine*, April 1931.

Report of the Ministry, Overseas Military Forces of Canada, 1918. London: Printed by Authority of the Ministry, Overseas Military Forces of Canada.

"Troop Convoy – How Canada Went to War in 1914," in *Crowsnest*, October, 1964. Summarizes the speech given by Rear-Admiral Hugh Pullen, RCN, Oct. 10th, 1964 to the Red Chevron Club of Ottawa (whose members were those who had gone overseas with the First Contingent – 32,000 men – of the Canadian Expeditionary Force in October, 1914). http://www.gwpda.org/naval/1cdncvy.htm, accessed March 28, 2002.

Weatherhead, Ted, "In Which Pooh Joins the Army and Lands in the Zoo," in *The Beaver*, October/November 1989.

"White River," article from the White River Heritage Museum.

"Winnie, Noted Canadian Black Bear Who Amused Londoners at Zoo Passes," *Winnipeg Free Press*, July 13, 1934.

B. Books

Alldis, Jim, *Animals As Friends, A Head Keeper Remembers London Zoo*. New York: Taplinger Publishing Co. Inc., 1973.

Brightwell, L. R., *The Zoo You Knew?* Oxford: Basil Blackwell, 1936.

French, Cecil (C.A.V. Barker and Ian K. Barker, eds.), *A History of the Canadian Army Veterinary Corps in the Great World War 1914-1918*. Guelph, Ontario: Crest Books, 1999.

Grainger, Jennifer, *Vanished Villages of Middlesex*. Toronto: Natural Heritage Books, 2002.

Houston, Mary, *White River – 100 Years, Pictorial History*. White River, Ontario: privately published, 1985.

Mainland, Leslie G., *Secrets of the Zoo*. London: S.W. Partridge & Co. Ltd., 1923.

Preston, Anthony, *Submarine Warfare: An Illustrated History*. San Diego, California: Thunder Bay Press, 1999.

Sidebotham, Helen, *Behind the Scenes at the Zoo*. London: Cassel and Company Ltd., 1925.

Sokoloski, Mia, *The Romance of the Captain and Winnie the Bear*. White River, Ontario: privately published, 1992.

Stefoff, Rebecca, *Bears*. New York: Benchmark Books, Marshall Cavendish, 2002.

Thwaite, Ann, *The Brilliant Career of Winnie-the-Pooh: The Story of A.A. Milne and His Writing for Children*. London: Methuen London, 1992.

C. Other Sources

Attestation Paper (for Harry Colebourn), National Archives of Canada.

Ontario Report, published by Ontario House, New York, Winter 1993.

Diaries of Harry Colebourn, Colebourn Collection, Provincial Archives of Manitoba.

Newspaper clippings and printouts provided by the Township of White River and by the White River Heritage Museum.

Statement of the Service of Major Harry Colebourn, National Archives of Canada.

Web Sites:

http://members.lycos.co.uk/blewholt/wwihorsedespatch/page6.html

http://www.fortgarryhorse.ca/HTML/winnie-the-bear.html

http://www.rootsweb.com/~cansk/CanadaInFlanders/ChapterI.html

http://www.gwpda.org/naval/1cdncvy.htm

http://www.peopleplayuk.org.uk/collections/object.php?search_result=true&object_id=577

http://www.londonzoo.co.uk/history/architecture.html

http://www.ku.edu/carrie/specoll/medical/vetindex.htm

http://www.museum.guelph.on.ca/mccraejohn.htm

http://www.pooh-corner.com/biomilne.html

http://lg.gov.mb.ca/speech/2001/mayjun/winniethepooh.html

Index

J.C. Penney, Bellevue, WA

Val (Valdine) Shushkewich was born and raised in Winnipeg and received a Bachelor of Arts degree from the University of Manitoba, majoring in history and anthropology. Research and writing have long been a personal interest, particularly in the world of nature. While visiting Assiniboine Park Zoo in Winnipeg, she was captivated by the statue of Winnie and Harry Colebourn, and was inspired to write about this very Canadian story.

Val currently lives in San Francisco, California, with her husband, Ken.